Don't Peek

The Diaries of a Teenage Girl

Marita A. Hansen

Copyright

Don't Peek

(The Diaries of a Teenage Girl)

Paperback Edition

Copyright 2013 © Marita A. Hansen

Edited by John Hudspith

Cover design © Arijana Karčić, Cover It! Designs

Cover Photography by Abdullah üsame Deniz

and sourced from http://depositphotos.com/

ISBN-13: 978-1492280910

ISBN-10: 1492280917

UK/Commonwealth English used due to the author being a New Zealander.

Other variations in spelling are also due to this.

Certain names and identifying details have been changed to protect the identity/privacy of the individuals concerned. The foreword further highlights this.

FOREWORD

I don't really want to say this, but here goes: *these are my teenage diaries.* Why don't I want to admit it? Because this boy-mad, angst-ridden teenager who wrote the messy scramble of words that I had to decipher was *very* embarrassing. After I read some of my diaries to my fifteen-year-old daughter, she called the younger version of myself 'adorkable' (adorable and dorky rolled into one), and she couldn't believe how innocent and oblivious I was, especially about boys. But there's a reason why I was like this. At the beginning of the diaries I was sixteen, never had a boyfriend, and had grown up in New Zealand during the 1970s and 80s as well as being raised in a strict culture (Yugoslav back then, Croatian now). Having come from a Catholic school, where only girls were in Form 1 and Form 2 (intermediate/middle school), I had very little knowledge of boys when I started public high school. On my first day, I had newly short hair (courtesy of my mother, which I wasn't happy about) and a way too long skirt (also courtesy of my mother, which again I wasn't happy about) and to make matters worse, the only friend I was starting high school with dumped me on my first day to be with her cousin's popular friends. Add to that an intensely shy girl, and you can pretty much guess my first year of high school was lonely and very awkward. But when I came

3

back the following year, my hair was longer, I'd learned a neat trick to hitch up my skirt so I didn't look like a dork, and, unbeknown to me, I had acquired two big assets that boys liked. But, I was still in the mindset of that girl who didn't have a clue as well as believing I was unattractive. Because of this, I inadvertently turned down a number of boys, which meant by the time I was sixteen I was aching for a boyfriend, screaming out in my head for one, whereas the boys were probably too scared to ask me out after my clueless blunders. So, this is where these diaries begin.

Just a couple of things before you start reading. As is the nature of diaries, I have not recorded all of the events that happened to me during this time; even some important ones have been left out. I have no idea why I didn't write about them, just that they weren't in there. Instead, I jotted down only what I felt like writing at the time, often using my diaries to vent or gush about whatever was on my mind. Yet, they do give a snapshot of my life and my thoughts from a viewpoint no one has ever seen. On the outside I was pretty calm, very polite, and didn't say that much, but as you will see, my mind didn't match the facade I put up.

Also, since everything in this book is real, I have changed names (of the people I know and the businesses I've worked for), even a couple of sports mentioned (not mine) as well as other references to protect people's identities. And in one extract, I have blanked out a name and changed how I know this person so I don't breach their privacy.

One last thing, I have included a few extras, such as letters and notes. So enjoy - or if you're like me, cringe at every word I wrote as an 'adorkable' teenager, because I certainly did, and if it wasn't for my daughter and my editor, who assured me my teenage self was worth reading about, these diaries would have remained hidden under my bed. So, thanks to them, and to the rest of my family, including my wonderful husband.

P.S. If you're a relative - DON'T PEEK!!!!

Diary 1988

WEDNESDAY
17
AUGUST

(Age 16)

I didn't play badminton that much the last time I went. I had a sore leg so I couldn't run around, which meant I mostly stayed in one place. My younger sister gave me the sore leg, because we got into a fight over earrings.

Sometimes I get upset when a guy I like doesn't show up to badminton, but I realise it isn't because of me, although I still get real hyper about it. And it doesn't help when the guys that do show aren't too happy. Devin was pissed off about something near the end of badminton. I tried to cheer him up. I don't think it was because he lost his games. He didn't appear to mind that. It was funny (not funny ha-ha, the other funny), because at the beginning he was trying to cheer me up. Though, I have a strange feeling he's pissed off due to me. I think he might have overheard me and Clara talking about Caleb. Possibly he's jealous that I like Caleb now. Or maybe he's upset because his bog-mouth friend Cooper was causing trouble.

I don't know what brought things on, but Cooper started asking me how Devin was and was teasing me about him, which was stupid because it was ages ago since I let Devin know I liked him, and I thought everyone knew that I went off him to Caleb. I guess not. Or maybe Devin was upset because it was the last night of badminton.

Anyway, I also went to karate the other night, which was real good, especially since Mike was there. His friend Liam was the instructor, because every brown belt has to take a class before they become a black belt. Mike, who's also a brown belt, was left to go round and check everyone was doing things correctly. Well, I know he knows my name and he acted quite friendly towards me. He showed me how to do a few techniques, then put a stick in front of me, which I was supposed to kick over, but I kept hitting it, which of course I wasn't supposed to do. I felt like a drongo. He just grinned.

When we were finished, I got changed and went out to wait for Dad. Mike and his friend Brent came out.

Brent was saying: "If I did that I would be like you." Then he glanced my way and said: "Oh no, you and her."

Mike replied: "I'll get you for that."

I think Brent was teasing Mike about me, although I didn't understand why, since I don't think Mike likes me. Maybe I'm wrong. Or maybe it could just mean he's taking more notice of me, it seems that way sometimes.

I got a video out today. Clara, one of my best friends, came over. The video was called 'National Anthem', and was about gymnastics. It was one of those movies that makes you want to do the sport, but I'm not good at gymnastics, I hated it when I did it in primary school. It's one of the few sports that I can't do well in, even though one of my primary teachers thought I was great at it, which I totally didn't get why. All she needed to do was watch me and she would have known how much I sucked at it. Once during gym class, she told all the other students to watch me do a cartwheel. She turned away to look at them just as I did this really pathetic cartwheel, and I mean REALLY pathetic, then turned back right after I'd finished. Next thing she's telling the class: "That's how you do a cartwheel." It was hilarious.

Anyway, forget about gymnastics, what I want is for Mum to let me continue doing karate, because I've got a feeling it's something I'm going to be good at. Usually at the beginning I'm disappointed when Mike doesn't show up, but as I get more into the lesson I'm soon very happy. It's so exhilarating. I love sport.

SUNDAY
28
AUGUST

I'm now in hospital after dislocating my little toe on my right foot at karate. It's hard to write, because my hand has got this thing in it that the drip goes through. Before I start writing about what happened today, I'll tell you about Thursday and so on.

On Thursday I went to work with Mum at the cafe. It was alright. Then at night I had karate. Mike wasn't there. I've got a feeling I'm going to be writing about him a lot. It's because I have a big crush on him, but it's different from the other crushes I've had. All I ever want to do is impress him or be near him. I can't help it. He's so nice. Let's face it, he's gorgeous! It's so confusing with boys. You never know whether they're interested in you or not, and when you let your feelings show, you've gone and put your foot in it again. Sometimes I wonder whether they're mocking or admiring me. I just wish for once it would be the second view.

All I want to do now is to improve myself, especially when it's the holidays. I want to return to school changed, so that boys (Mike in particular) will like me. I could grow my hair long. That would make me look different. I feel like my features are changing. I feel more confident in my looks. I don't exactly know why, but I do. It could be that I'm growing more mature and into a young woman. I reckon I could look really pretty. I sometimes feel I could be a model. I just need to be done up that's all. Yeah, because I have a nice skin colour, like I'm tanned all year, and I've got big eyes that could be used to my advantage, and I've got a nice oval face. And the colour of my eyes could be brought out nicely, especially with dark eyeliner and mascara. And my lips are just right, while my hair is real feathery, especially when it's washed. I could be real Spanish looking if I put dark makeup on and curl my hair. I reckon I could be a model, and I'm going to prove it. And I'm going to try my best to get Mike!

But, back to Thursday's karate. It went good. Boy, do I love that sport. We did some more fighting and a lot of exercises. That young black belt is real cute, his name's Ryan. But guess what? I'm saving all my love for Mike.

On Friday I stayed home, on Saturday Mum, Nina (my younger sister), and I went to Manukau City. It was good. Mum got the Yugoslav music tape from Aussie today. Dad got a surprise this morning when Mum put it on.

I'm getting distracted again, so AGAIN back to karate! I got up as usual on Sunday (today), made breakfast in bed for Nina's birthday (she's now 14), had my own breakfast, then rode off to karate. We started the session with a warm up and stretches, Jeremy took it, he's a green belt. Then we all went to one end of the hall and started playing a game just like bullrush. After a couple of times running up and down, dodging the middle person, who was trying to touch us out of the game, I collided with an orange belt and wacked my foot against the floor. It was then that I saw my little toe was bleeding and my bone was protruding out of the skin. I went into shock and wasn't able to tell anyone what had happened, although I tried to. So I went to rinse my toe in the girls' loos. Then Nick, a brown belt, and the lead black belt, came over to see what was wrong. They saw that my toe was broken and Nick went off to get changed so he could take me to the hospital. Meanwhile, I had my foot up on a desk with the black belt talking to me, while I'm looking attentively at Mike, wondering whether he had noticed me. My toe wasn't really hurting, well, not that much, just majorly pulsating.

Nick came back and the black belt carried me to Nick's car. Nick then took me to the hospital. He phoned Mum, and stayed with me until Mum and Dad came, then he returned to get my gear and bike, so he could take them home for me. Nick's nice, he's really friendly.

I got my toe put back in place, but before they could do that they had to put it to sleep with an injection which HURT LIKE CRAZY! It felt like the doctor had stabbed the needle right through my toe. I didn't watch when he put my bone back in place, because my toe looked horrible and floppy. I hadn't actually broken it, it was dislocated. It felt heaps better after, because it had stopped pulsating, which was more of a nuisance than a pain, <u>unlike</u> that needle. Another thing that is a nuisance is the thing in my left hand for the drip. It limits my writing ability, because I'm unable to lean on it.

Mum and Dad left when I was moved to my room, but Dad came back later around 6:15pm. He brought me my things, and stayed for a while. I changed into a nightie before Dad arrived, which was more comfortable. I haven't been out of bed since this morning now.

There was this lady earlier in the same hospital room as me who is 93, but she wasn't very well. I think she had just come back from theatre. There's another old lady here who is 83, she isn't well either. It's strange how people treat the elderly like children, especially when they can't do very much. The old lady across from me is treated like a little child. I feel sorry for her, but I suppose she's lived a happy life. Her family were really nice; the little boy with them was so adorable. There has been a lot of kids here today, visiting their grandparents. Each one of the ladies in my room had a small child visiting them.

Now I've finished telling you about what happened to me, I still feel like writing. I feel like spilling out everything. Even though I'm in hospital, I feel great. All I want to do is to start right back from where I left off. I just feel so full of life. I should stop writing now, because it's getting hot and late.

Man, I just can't hold in what I feel. So, before I write any more "Good night."

SATURDAY
3
SEPTEMBER

I'm out of hospital now so will tell you what happened over the past week, but before I do that, I want to say one thing: I have no idea why I wrote all that stuff about me being a model, because I was an IDIOT! And a blind one who obviously doesn't look in the mirror enough. Idiot. Man, I should cross it out, but I suppose no one's going to read it, so I can't be bothered. Anyway, they have to decipher the great mess called my writing. Ha-ha. Suckers.

Back to writing – messily. On Monday one of the black belts came to visit me. He's going to be the second highest black belt soon. He exercises so much, especially in aerobics. Then Mum and my younger sister stayed for a while, and later on, about 4 pm, my older sister came (Lauren is 22). She told me she will be engaged in a couple of months when she gets the ring. The reason she isn't engaged right now is because her boyfriend and her are saving up for a car. I'm not supposed to tell anyone until it's official, and when it's official, a year later they will be married. Isn't that great? Her boyfriend is a million times better than her last one. She reckons so too. She doesn't exactly have great taste in guys. When I was younger I used to tease her about one of them, but that was my job as a younger sister, he-he. Although I was a jerk for doing it, especially since the guy had a stutter. I can't remember how old I was, but whenever I said his name to her I would say 'M-M-M-Mason', mainly because every time he phoned for my sister he would say his name this way, so I would repeat it. There was also this advertisement where the singer said that name for some type of housing product, so sometimes I would sing it too. Told you I was a jerk.

The girl in the bed next to me knew my older sister from Stanton School. She broke her ankle when she fell off her horse.

Anyway, when my sister left the hospital after a long talk with me, I was wheeled over in my bed to the TV room, where I watched the Emmy awards until they were finished. After that I was taken back to my room and went to sleep.

The next day I stayed in hospital until about 3:00 pm, which was when Mum came and picked me up to take me home. I got my crutches and I can use them well.

Clara visited me on Tuesday. Obviously, I didn't go to karate, even to watch. Nothing much to say about Wednesday and Thursday. On Friday, Mum and I got up early to go get my toe cleaned and strapped. It was real quick. Then we went to Shanton for a quick look at clothes, then back home. Mum left for work after that. Nothing much happened that day, except Mum got me Dad's Father's Day present and card, and some art stuff.

I just rang Caleb (from badminton) to see whether he wanted to see 'Short Circuit' but he said he'd seen it with his little brother. This may be true, but I'm getting frustrated with boys. Whatever I do about them, nothing ever seems to come out of it. And I'm getting fed up, and now I'm thinking about it, I'm going to do a scene to make boys interested in me, and I know I can do it too, because I reckon Caleb did like me, so why not? I read a book about this girl who was too shy around boys for them to take notice of her, so her friends set up scenes to make her popular. She had a schedule for each day of the week to get boys' attention, like in some classes she would drop a pencil (for a boy to pick up), or she rang up a boy about homework or asked them innocent questions just to make them notice her, and it worked. So why shouldn't it work for me too? And also I'm on crutches, so boys have got to be a little curious.

Schedule for what good-looking boys are in my classes:

Monday
Bio – Kenneth?
Art – ?
Computers – More than one.

Typing – Matthew??

Study – Matthew. Kane!

I can smile a lot and say "Hi." In Study I can ask to borrow something, then smile – most innocently. What a joke. It's fun having a diary, where you can write way-out ideas. The only thing I'm worried about is someone else reading it.

Another idea is I can walk, or in my case, hobble past Mike a lot to catch his interest and I can smile. Most people say my smile is cheeky, mischievous. Though, it can get me into trouble sometimes because I often smile when I'm getting told off. But I can't help it, it's a nervous reaction. Not my fault they think I'm being cheeky.

Who else can I work on? Even 5th formers, fourths are a bit too young at my age, maybe when they're older, but I doubt it. It's got to be someone special like Mike! This last term has got to be my lucky term. I hope!

I can be really friendly. I should be nicer to Jill though, because she doesn't have a lot of friends. I reckon the way she acts is just a show when she is around people. A lot of people are like that. They're all show. That gives me an idea. Well, not really, but I just remembered Robert Jenkins. I think he liked me in 5th form, so there's another guy who's alright. I know this term is going to be different and I'm going to prove it. I'm going to set a goal and get what I want. I can change everything. I'll be a whole lot friendlier, talk to more people, make them notice me. I'll start straight away when I get to school. Mum will be giving me a ride because of my foot, which means my younger sister and Shena will also get a lift. So, when I get to school I can smile at everyone, be really friendly and jokey, just to make people – boys – notice me. I need to boost my self-esteem. I am DEFINITELY GOING TO HAVE A BOYFRIEND VERY SOON!!

FRIDAY
9
SEPTEMBER

(Age 17)

I am just so fed up with my younger sister, all she ever does is try to annoy me and she's very good at it. I wish she would just quit it; it really gives me a headache and makes me so frustrated. You just can't win with her.

I had my birthday on Wednesday – Mum, my younger sister, and I went to see 'Short Circuit 2' and I got some real nice earrings from Clara, she also gave me some stockings. And prior to this, on Father's Day, we all went to my grandparents' place for a relations' gathering. I got my present from Aunty Tiana there.

There's nothing much else I want to say about what happened over the past week, but I would like to write down what I feel. I'm getting excited about school, but I still want it to be holidays. I just have to make a change for myself. Today, I was looking for clothes to wear to school on Monday, because I want to look good like everyone else. I want to feel good about myself. I feel like washing my hair now, but I won't, because it's better to wash it on Sunday so it'll look nice for school. I wonder what will happen there – whether it'll be the same old frustrating stuff or a nice change for once with a bit of excitement, like two guys going after me, and both of them are gorgeous. Wouldn't that be great? And I wouldn't know which one to pick, although I would probably choose one from the other. In America they date more than one person at the same time. I reckon it should be one at a time, whether you are going steady or not.

I hope that things will change at school for me, meaning I get to go out with boys, so I've got to get my plan working, meaning the schedule for getting them to notice me. I don't want to chicken out or anything. I'm seventeen now, and I think it's high time for me to have a boyfriend, so I'm going to try my hardest to prove to Mike or any other boy that I'm worthy of being their girlfriend.

There's going to be a lot of smiling going on from Monday at school.

SATURDAY
10
SEPTEMBER

My brother is coming tonight (he's 20). He's bringing presents for me and my younger sister, since our birthdays are close together. I think I'm getting a record voucher. If I'm right, I would probably buy either Kylie Minogue's or Debbie Gibson's record.

I want to change my bedroom around, but since the holidays went so quick I didn't have the time, so in the Christmas break I'm going to totally redecorate it, and I've got heaps of ideas to make arty things for my room, like halving a car and joining it to the wall. I'll have the windscreen area as a mirror and the seat in the car will open up to be a drawer, and the front trunk will also be used for storage, and it will be covered in soft material. I don't know what the material is called, maybe velvet or something like that. Crushed velvet? I've got heaps of other ideas, but I don't feel like writing them all down, but the car is the first on my list.

I better do my homework now.

Continued—

'21 Jump Street' was so cool tonight. Man, Johnny Depp is super gorgeous. He was acting undercover as the tough guy.

He wore a bandana around his head and was in denim. If a guy like him was at my school, man, every girl would be after him. And seeing someone like that makes me want to be cool, and it makes me want to be liked by boys. I wish I could go to school wearing a hat or a bandana, but I just don't have the guts to do it. Maybe in the third term my image will change, and I will become more well-known.

I wore Clara's hat all day. I didn't bother mingling with boys, but I promise I will tomorrow. Anyway, I saw Mike. He is just so-o-o-o gorgeous. I really want to go out with him. Today he was wearing a black hooded sweatshirt and his black jacket. He's got a real nice bod too, actually the truth is – he's got a gorgeous bod and everything that comes with it. The problem now is that I won't be going to karate so I can't see him, and at school, the only time I see him is when I go out of my way to the art room at roll call, and also if I'm lucky I may see him after or before school. But I can't get him to notice me. It's really annoying. What do I have to do to get his attention? And dislocating my toe doesn't count.

Well, he saw me with Clara's hat on, but he didn't show any interest. Actually, I wasn't looking at him straight, only out of the corner of my eye, so I couldn't really tell what he was doing.

Day 5 tomorrow

English
Bio
Art
Liberal Studies

<u>Computers</u>

Home

I used to make up a list of all the classes Gabriel Norton had with me or near me. I really liked him; he liked me a lot in 4th form, I only wish I had believed him. I might have gone out with him if I had. I was such a moron, but how was I supposed to know he liked me that much? Okay, he called me spunky and kept looking at me, but I wasn't used to being noticed by guys, so my stupid brain didn't register it. I realise it now, but back then I didn't have a clue. No boys paid me attention in 3rd form, then all of a sudden in 4th form three guys in my class were paying me attention. I didn't believe it, because two of them were in my class the previous year and they never paid me attention then. And when Gabriel did, I felt flattered, but I never really thought he was serious, just thought it was all a tease, until he found out (from one of my so-called friends) that I had sent a stupid note to an older boy (which led to nothing, because I didn't sign it). But I wasn't going out with Gabriel, and I didn't really understand how much he liked me. And anyway, I don't understand boys, they confuse me. If he thought I was his girlfriend, he should have asked me out, because how was I supposed to know otherwise. I DON'T UNDERSTAND BOYS!

Back to now. I can't make a list of classes for Mike, because he isn't in any of mine since he's a 2nd year 5th former.

Everything is happening so quick, it's confusing. I'm really busy. I got my poetry project handed in on time, but only because I stayed up way past 11:00 (obviously pm) to do it, and worked on it all through my other subjects and lunchtime just to get it finished and out of my hair.

The Olympics are on tomorrow at 12:30, which is really exciting. 'Teen Wolf' the movie is on at night, and so is '21 Jump Street' with Johnny Depp, which is my favourite programme at the moment.

Mum brought some perming solution home today for Nina and her. I'm having thoughts about my hair being done too.

I can't wait till the Christmas holidays. School finishes on November the 18th. I could do what I like, it would be so choice! I'm going to totally redecorate my room, and I'll be back at karate by then.

44 days left of school.

Mike is gorgeous, but I have to control my feelings and keep it cool. I know I write about him a lot, (but) the reason for this is that I want to talk to someone. I'm not only ranting and raving about him in my diary, but I'm letting my feelings out to cool off. I need to talk to someone, like I said before. I need a boyfriend. I get so lonely sometimes. Well, not really lonely, but I feel like there's something missing in me. Clara has a boyfriend, Mike (not my Mike obviously) and she's really happy. Well, it makes up for her first boyfriend Samuel. I don't know why she went out with him; she must have liked him a weenie bit, even though she says she can't stand him, and calls him names.

I saw Mike (my one) walking home from school today. I reckon he doesn't like me at all. It's just a bad feeling.

Mike's description:

Gorgeous bright blue eyes, slim, and the right height (taller than me). Dark brown wavy hair, a gorgeous style. Gorgeous bod.

I've just got to get him out of my mind, unless by some way-out miracle, which is most highly unlikely, he asks me out. To get him out of my head, I've got to think of other things, like concentrate on work. I've got 3 projects to do by the end of the month, lots of tests and an exam for Typing, which will be 2 hours long.

<u>Projects</u>

Bio – Birds (rare).

Typing – Folio (on myself).

Computers – Essay on any topic to do with computers.

I need to go to the library to return some books and to get some out for Bio and Computers, as well as get other information. I could work down there – study – do homework.

Well, good night.

3 more weeks until I start karate again. I can't wait. I really want to go; it's so different without it. I wonder what I will do when I get back - because of my toe. Also, I will be missing badminton for 3 weeks, since it starts tomorrow. I hope that Caleb won't turn up when I'm not there. That would ruin everything.

I want to write a book. It could be about this girl who's got this crush on this boy at her karate class. I might have to change that, because if someone reads it, it could state the obvious. Anyway, back to the story, this girl also goes to badminton and she likes a guy there as well. She gets her friends to ask him out for her and he says yes, but they don't get together because he has a job on the only night they can meet. She gets so confused and school becomes frustrating, and all she can wait for is the Christmas holidays. Also, she misses karate because of a dislocated toe, and badminton also. She's unsure of herself and wonders whether she will ever get a boyfriend.

AND, she wants to ask the boy from karate to go to a school ball – her friends do it for her. She feels embarrassed around him sometimes, but goes out of her way just to see him, without him noticing her, because she has an art class in his form room.

PLUS, her best friend has a new boyfriend and she feels even more lonely when she sees them together, and sometimes is annoyed because her friend is always with her boyfriend and his friends, and she's not too keen on this.

This could make a great book. I could write it in the holidays, and when I get more time I could also do my art sculptures after it. I reckon the story's a great idea, and would be suited to the teenage public. They would be interested in it. I'll read more teenage books in the holidays when I have time. I don't think it would be good for the adult public. When I grow up, I could write one for them, but right now I prefer teenage books.

I could write a book like Victoria Holt. Mum could read it, because she likes those books a lot. I could study her books and also Barbara Cartland's ones. I've never read a Cartland book before, but I know Victoria Holt's books are good.

I could write it about a princess who runs away from home because of her sister's jealousy of her beauty. She's scared for her life, so she leaves behind her childhood darling, who her sister fancies. The princess then travels into the country with a new identity to protect herself. She comes to a small village which is run by this big manor that has mysterious owners, and one who she falls in love with. But meanwhile her other lover goes in search for her, but not knowing why she ran away he leads the main character's sister to her, who is mysteriously beautiful, but very wicked, and so all three become entangled in the mystery of the manor house, and its secret murders. The older sister dies in the end and the owner of the house goes missing – he murdered the older sister, thinking she was the other one. And the childhood sweetheart saves the good sister's life and they go back to her father's palace and get married. There could be a sequel to it. That would be great.

SATURDAY
24
SEPTEMBER

Man, am I tired. It's a Saturday morning. I shouldn't have stayed up so late last night. My toe's getting better, and from tomorrow I've got two weeks before I can do anything – sport, I mean. I've got to hand in a biology project next Friday, so I need to do it this weekend, then during the week I have to finish photocopying all the information I've got on the subjects. I also got an English project to hand in, so that will be done during lunch time and after school at the library. And then there is the Typing resume project due. Heaps of homework! I don't really have any time to be bored. Well, I know I won't be bored during the Christmas holidays. I'm counting the days. I've got so much stuff I want to do then. This year, I've never been bored in the holidays, because I had lots of work and the time left was taken up quickly.

18th of November is the day we get off school, which isn't that great, because now I've got to wait approximately 39 days before school is finished – I think that's near enough correct.

I will be missing another karate lesson and Tuesday's karate lessons till I go back, I think. I can't wait. I played badminton yesterday, doubles. We won one game. All I could do was hobble around the court doing my best. I don't have to go to the doctor's anymore since I can change the dressing myself.

Clara's birthday is coming up, so I have to get her something. I've already got my mum's present; her birthday is a week from Tuesday.

I will be missing another two weeks of badminton. I hope I won't be missing Caleb. Devin might be there too.

(Sorry, I'm writing in such a mess. I'll try to tidy it up.)

I remember when I had badminton last, these guys who knew Devin were teasing me about an old crush I had on him. I don't know why, because he's cute and all, and I would go out with him if he asked me, but I wouldn't go barmy over him. It happened a long time ago. He's alright, I suppose. Though, I shouldn't have talked about Caleb around him, because he looked a bit glum and I was being stupid about Caleb like that. If Caleb wants to go out with me, it will happen and if he doesn't then too bad. The same thing goes for Mike and Devin, because I'm sick of worrying about it and trying to speed things up. I don't like being made a fool of, and I won't take it. I'm not going to ask any boys out anymore! Unless I am their girlfriend officially! Well, I better go and do my jobs, so I can start on my homework as soon as possible and finish it quickly.

I'm going to someone's birthday party on Saturday at 7:30. I don't even know who the person is. You see, Clara invited me because she knew the person from her Youth group. It's at the hall, next to the Methodist church. I don't even know what a Methodist is.

Today I felt like such a jerk. Since I like Mike Nicholls, when it was time to go home, I walked slow, because I wanted to see him, but him and his friends were late, so I went all over the place to give them a chance to catch up. I am NEVER going to do that again!! I felt like a real jerk, he probably didn't notice me. Probably lucky he didn't because I was a mess. From now on, I am just going to walk home normally! I also felt like a jerk at lunch after art when I was drawing, because when I looked up from drawing he turned around. I got the feeling that he thought I was looking at him. That happened twice and I didn't do it on purpose. It wasn't my fault, it was an accident. That also happened once before when I had a crush on Gabriel Norton, and it wasn't my fault then either, it was just a coincidence.

I saw Mike a lot today because he went to his locker, which is near mine and he also walked past to go to a class. It looked like he was looking at me; I felt embarrassed and lowered my head. I must be more confident in myself!

I have my Bio project to hand in on Monday, an English project tomorrow, an art project on Wednesday, the Typing resume for Thursday, and the art folio to be handed in soon, but I don't know when.

FRIDAY
30
SEPTEMBER

(Written on paper and found in diary)

<u>During English</u>

I've got 2 more weeks before I can go back to doing sport (properly) again – karate and badminton. Mike will be at karate. I have been seeing him a lot lately since he's been going to his locker and classes, which means he has to walk past me. It's just been this week that I've seen him a lot, I don't know why.

I can't wait till I go back to karate and badminton. At badminton I might see Caleb again. I hope I do. I might even see Devin too. I just want to know who's going.

At karate Mike will be there, as I said before. He is just so gorgeous, (and) I really want to go out with him. It would be neat if I could get into his group. I never knew this group before this year, and it's mainly because of karate that I know who they are now. I wouldn't know who they were if I didn't go to karate. I wish Mike would notice me. He probably does actually, but I reckon he reckons I'm a jerk who's got a crush on him, which is true, because I do have a crush on him and I feel like a jerk around him. It's not fair, why doesn't anyone I like, like me. I should have taken the opportunity with Gabriel

Norton. I could have gone out with him (if I had a brain!). I also had some other guys every so often interested in me, but they were either too young, too short, or creepy old guys (shiver), or just jerks, like one guy who used to bug me when I was fourteen. He got a friend to ask me if I liked him in class, but I didn't like him like that, though he was nice enough (at that point!). Anyway, the unfortunate bit was that the guy who was asking for him was someone who I actually had a crush on at the time, so I was embarrassed (and annoyed), so I sort of was trying to ignore his question because I didn't want to answer it. But the guy didn't take a hint and eventually I said no, but I must have said it too softly because he continued asking until I snapped and yelled "No!" in the middle of class. I felt so-o-o bad about doing that, but he was driving me nuts. Though, I paid for it afterwards (still am) because the guy's friends started teasing me and calling me 'sloppy box'. And I do know what it means! But how can I be a sloppy box if I haven't had sex let alone kissed a guy?! Jerks. I don't go around calling guys names just because I got turned down. Plus, the guy who liked me smacked my butt at skating. I should've punched him, like I punched his mate for slapping me when I made him drop his books. I probably shouldn't have done that, but still, he shouldn't have slapped me. Though, my punch made him cry. Guess I was made for karate.

All up, it's really depressing not having gone out with anyone. It gets lonely. All these pretty girls have got it made, why can't I have a little bit of opportunity (now)? Sometimes, or most of the time, I reckon guys think I'm weird. Well, not exactly, but it feels like all I need to do is to look at them and they think I'm staring. It's because of my big eyes. That's what I reckon anyway, though I hope they don't think that.

I've got to pick up my art after English, so I can do some work on it over the weekend. I will probably see Mike when I get it. I hope he doesn't think I'm following him around.

SUNDAY
2
OCTOBER

I'm setting myself a goal – I definitely want to go to the Olympics, for sure. It's going to be my dream. I'm no longer going to think or say I'm going to train, but I will! Everyone's got to set a goal and the Olympics are mine. I think Spain will be my main goal. I've got two years to train, after my toe's better. I'm going to get stuck right into it. Cycling will definitely be my sport. I really love to do canoeing, but I haven't got a canoe or anything to take it to the beach. I've got a bike, and when I was watching the cycling on TV I thought it looked like a sport that I would be good at, and I'm certainly going to try my best. No goal is too high if a person sets their mind to it, but they must try their best and that is what I'm going to do. I'm going to try my upmost to be part of the Olympics. Just watching it can make you shiver (in a good way, not in the creepy old guy way). All those people from practically every nation there with you, it's so brilliant – special. I would treasure that forever. Oh, I would really love it. I've got another month and a half of school left and when my toe's better I've got to train so hard. I'm not going to check myself out of this opportunity – I'm going to live up to this goal. I'm going to fulfil it, and it will be because I did my best, and I pushed myself. No one can stop me now!

That last part sounds like a Queen song.

MONDAY
3
OCTOBER

I'm still determined to be in the Olympics. I don't know whether there are any cycling clubs around, but next year I'm going to enter the triathlete's club – mainly for the cycling, but the running part will also be good, although the swimming section will be hard, because I'm a pretty hopeless swimmer.

I'm going to get a pair of those cycling pants, they're going to be excellent, and I will train in them, because I definitely want to go to Barcelona. That would be glorious if I could get into that team. I could also train for the Commonwealth Games in Auckland, and if I get anywhere in that I could get a sponsor for the Spanish Olympics. Wouldn't that be great? It would be marvellous.

I thought about my dream all day and I'm really going to do it. I'm going to take on this goal and it's not going to be just babbling, but action. I would have it for life if I did well in cycling, or any other sport come to think of it.

I can't go to badminton tonight because of my toe, but I will definitely be going next week. Also, I will be starting back at karate soon. I need to be very fit and any sport will help.

I'm getting distracted by boys again. Why is it always that I can't keep my mind off them? At school I'm always looking out for Mike, and when I go to badminton it would be for Caleb and if he's not there maybe Devin. Well, can't they just leave my head and let me concentrate on something else for once? Actually, the only thing that rids them from my mind are my thoughts on the Olympics. That is my idea of a glorious dream.

THURSDAY
6
OCTOBER

I think I saw Caleb today, I'm not sure though. It was when I was walking home from school. A van came around the corner and it looked like Caleb was in it. It really did, but I'm not positive. I hope he will be at badminton on Monday. I really do like him a lot. I hope he still likes me.

I will be going back to karate on Sunday. I saw Mike today, he is just so gorgeous. I wish I wasn't so strung up on boys, but everything about him is perfect. Oh man, I just can't stop thinking about him or going off in a daze. I pray that I will get a boyfriend soon. I really need one, because it gets lonely without one. I'm 17 now and never had a date. I need to know a boy closely, like someone you could confide in, maybe joke with, be with, have fun with.

I'm seeing a movie tomorrow for Liberal Studies. One thing about some movies is that they arouse you, make you feel special or different. Music does that to you too. It makes you want to change, show the world what you are like. I just can't stop thinking about having a boyfriend; it's probably why I write in this diary. I'm doing it again! Writing about one thing, then suddenly changing the topic to boys. It's annoying, but I can't help it. In church the other day the priest was saying that you're not whole until you get the other half of you, which will be your partner for life. I think he's right, and I really want that partner, I need him.

Even though I'm talking about boys again, I haven't forgotten about my cycling dreams. I still really want to go to the Olympics. It's just another dream like having a boyfriend, and I'm going to have both.

You just wait till school finishes and my training begins, I'm going to return to school in the 7th form as another, better person. 7th form is going to be the ultimate, I'm going to do things that I've never even dreamed of – you'll see. I'm going to prove to everyone that I'm special. Everyone is special, but I'm going to show just how special I can be in my own unique way.

FRIDAY
7
OCTOBER

(Written on a piece of paper during Bio class)

I should bring my diary to school, especially for Bio since it's so boring. I really don't know why I took it, since I don't like Science. I can't wait till there's no more Bio whatsoever; and a few other subjects too. Some of them are just so bad, like computers. I have computers instead of Art for 3rd period today because the periods are swapped over. It's a pain really.

Mum will take me home after school. I hope I can get my art pad, so I can do my graphic project. Also, I have some English homework that has drawings in it, about 'The Man from Snowy River'. We're going to see that movie on Monday. I've seen it before, but that was ages ago. I can't really remember it except for who acted as the main character's girlfriend. Though, I remember it was a good movie.

I'll be able to go back to karate on Sunday, so I'll have to miss church in the morning. I wonder whether anything will be different when I go back to karate or not. There will probably be people who have gone up a grade, most likely the green belts. I hope I will be alright doing the exercises because of my toe. I'll be alright for badminton, because it's not done in bare feet, and it's only running about, not kicking or doing push ups.

SATURDAY
8
OCTOBER

Me, Mum, and Nina are going to Manukau now. I'm going to fill out a Denny's application form so I can work there. I hope I can get the job because it's really close and handy to get to. It's like the restaurant Hungry Horse. Now I'm 17 I've got a better chance of getting the job.

I can't wait until badminton on Monday. I had a dream last night that Caleb came to school looking for me, and when I saw him he ran away, but I ran after him and caught up, and then we both sat on the same bench that Mike sits on and we talked. Dreams are weird because we played cards. I can also remember small details, like my skirt was that long one, and Amy saw Caleb and recognised him as my boyfriend, and she has never seen him before. And his sisters were there too, but I can't remember what they were doing. Again, it was weird, but dreams are always like that.

I must go now – to Manukau.

New Zealand is currently losing Rugby League to Australia and will probably lose it altogether at the end. It has really pissed me off, I am so mad at it. I feel like going out on my bike and cycling all my anger out. It is so aggravating because they're dropping the ball, the idiots. I'm going to start training straight away because this has pissed me off so much. I'm going to have to pump up my tyre.

I'm going to get my cycling pants on Tuesday. I think cycling's going to be great, and I'm going to cycle up hills heaps. Really push myself. I'm giving boys a back seat now because they make me so angry too. I'm sick and tired of them ignoring me and I heard Mike call me the girl with the hairy legs. It's not my fault Mum won't let me shave them, and anyway, it's none of his or the other boys' business. All they want to do is make some stupid remarks to hurt me. And they think they're cool! Well, they're not! They're stupid idiots.

I think I might ride to school tomorrow and back, and tell Shena I won't be walking with her unless it rains. I feel like running now, but I can't because of my toe. I won't be allowed to. What shall I do now? I don't feel like watching any more rugby league. But just as I write this New Zealand has got a try. It may make us feel a little bit better, but I think it's too late. The conversion has been missed, so it's 25 to 8. It's far too late to win.

I'm a bit mad about karate also, because I can't do much with my toe like this, it's really annoying. I can't wait until tomorrow due to badminton. Actually, it's not really badminton, but Caleb. I really want to see him. Even though I said before about giving guys a back seat, I can't help it. Just watching Corey Feldman earlier on TV reminds me of Caleb. I always get my hopes up too high with guys. I know I shouldn't. Caleb probably won't even be there tomorrow and of course I will be disappointed. What can you expect from me? To be happy about it? I just want to see him, not Mike, not anyone else, but Caleb. I just want to see him.

The end result of the Rugby League game is New Zealand 12, Australia 25. What a disappointment. Man, I really want to see Caleb. I know I'm raving about him, but I have to get my mind off rugby league and on to a good subject. I'm sick of school now; I just want to get out of it. I know I'm complaining a lot, but I've got to get it out of my system, so I don't cause conflict with someone else.

I'm going to blast my eardrums out with music. Music seems to calm me down, so I don't think of annoying things. This diary also calms me down. It really helps to get all my feelings out. You could say it's a substitute for a person or a boyfriend, because I don't have a boyfriend, so I can't get my feelings out and I stuff it all up and get real upset. I'm writing really fast here and I don't want to stop. I never had a diary quite like this one before. My other diaries were stupid ones. They just stated what had happened and it was in an immature way. They were childish, whereas this one has more character and depth to it.

I love sport and I'm not going to desert my dream for Olympic gold in cycling. If Bruce Kendall, Ian Ferguson, Paul McDonald and other great Kiwis can get an Olympic medal, why can't I? I'm great, aren't I? To succeed you've got to be confident in yourself or else you will fail, and no one wants to fail, everyone wants to be a success. Don't they? And I'm going to succeed, aren't I?

I'm going to show everyone that I'm not just a stupid girl but a terrific one. I want to show them how special I am. I'm not going to be a singer, actor or anything stupid like that, but I'm still going to be a star. A star of sport and specialness.

I'm really going to succeed and win my way to satisfaction.

SUNDAY
16
OCTOBER

I can't believe it; I actually shaved my legs, I did it without Mum knowing. I snuck into the bathroom and locked the door, then used one of Dad's shavers. I can't believe it! I know it isn't a big deal for you or anyone else, but I have been teased for having hairy legs (well, only once when I heard Mike) and now I haven't any. I just can't believe it! Now I can go to school in skirts and do P.E. in shorts without feeling so conscious about them.

Mike was at karate today. I felt like such an idiot when he had to repeat a question twice. He speaks softly, so I couldn't hear him. I just felt like a dick going:

"What?"

"What?"

Well, too bad, it's over and I can't change it.

The black belts are doing their grading next Saturday, it goes on for 24 hours. There's karate on Saturday and Sunday from 9am-12pm for everyone else. I don't know whether I'll go on Saturday. Dunno. Well, I don't seem to want to write anymore. But just one thing: I've finished my art poster for Waiheke Island and I reckon it's great.

P.S. My typing exam was a disaster, so I don't want to talk about that mishap.

WEDNESDAY
19
OCTOBER

(Written on a note)

I'm doing Bio now and then I have Typing. I don't want to go to Typing, since we're getting back our exams, which I did terribly in, because I didn't realise there were more questions on the back of the paper. I'm afraid I am going to get an awful mark, which is bad since it's worth 50% for the whole year.

We've only got 4 and a half weeks left of school now. It's going so fast. I've got karate tomorrow night for the first time in ages. I really have a big crush on Mike Nicholls. I hate calling it a crush, but I can't think of anything else to call it. Boy, wouldn't I be in a mess if someone read my diary. It would be shameful.

(Typed on a different piece of paper during Typing class)

I am typing this now because I'm frustrated with my typing exam mark, which was 38%. Also, for once in typing I don't know what to do. I should continue writing on the sheet that I used for biology, but I like typing things out. This is my last period for the day and thank goodness for that.

I am sick and tired of not having a boyfriend. I haven't even been out with a boy yet, isn't that stupid. I know who I

53

would like to go out with and you can see who it is in my diary. Mike Nicholls. Boys must think I'm weird. It's not fair. All the other girls get to go out with boys while I stay home. When I went to Rainbow's End with some friends last year I was really left out because I didn't have a boyfriend. Well, that's how I felt. Why can't I have a guy who like, likes me for once. I'm not asking for too much am I? I think Caleb liked me because he said he wanted to go out with me, but what happened? I didn't see him again. It's just so frustrating and unfair. I wish Mike would like me, but I guess I'm asking for too much. Sometimes I feel that guys mock me. It isn't funny. Why can't they be nice to me? I'm also fed up with who I'm sitting with at school. Clara's alright, because she's my best friend, but Jill is a pain in the neck, she always makes me annoyed. Also, all Clara does is sit with Mike (her Mike, not mine) in the Science rooms. She never wants to do anything. I wish that I was in a group like the one Mike (my one) is in, but it's only wishes, not reality.

I still want to be a cyclist and go to the Olympics. I will be training in the summer holidays. I've got karate tomorrow. I hope that I will soon be able to go every time. I can't do this yet because my toe is not completely better from the accident.

Well, I better finish typing this, because the bell is going to ring any minute now.

I just had karate. It went from 9 am to 12 pm. Mike was there. I keep on thinking that I always do something wrong when he's around. I mean, I always want to impress him. I hate to write this in the diary now because I'm just writing the same things over and over again. It's annoying. Nothing ever seems to happen.

Night time

I've got a cold and it's a pain in the neck or more accurately the throat. Also, I have my art piece to finish, but I think it's too cluttered for reproduction. I hope not, because it works real good, and there isn't enough time left to do much else. Plus, I've got a test on Tuesday for Biology to study for. It's genetics and all that stuff.

Well, enough of that, I want to talk about MIKE (well, not exactly). Anyway, I really want him but I don't have much luck with boys. He is just so-o-o-o-o gorgeous. I wish that he would like me, because I really like him a lot. I want to know what he feels. He is a nice person and everything else. I want to be able to talk to him, see his views. I want to help him with his homework and if he wants to, he can help me. I want to go on bike rides with him. Have fun with him. Be with him. I only wish he would feel the same way about me. I never wrote anything like this in my previous diaries, about a boy, that is. Still, it's really good to get things like this out. It's better to open up somehow, rather than to keep it all bottled up inside. I can sometimes get too inward or shy with my emotions. I know I've got to share them with another person, and since I don't have another person right now the diary substitutes until I can get someone I can relate to, be in love with. I want that person to be Mike.

I know I'm sounding a bit too serious here, but I need to write. I need to let it out. Boy, if Mike knew about this book and what I felt about him – I'm just speechless.

I wish he would pay more attention to me. I wish he would smile at me at school or even say hi. And most of all, I wish he would ask me to go out and around, or even his friends can ask me for him, so any which way I still get to go out with him. Because I know how hard it is to ask someone out.

A wish: Please, Mike, will you ask me out?

What will happen?

MONDAY
24
OCTOBER

I don't have school today because it's Labour Day, so it's a long weekend. I've got my Bio test tomorrow, so I've got to study heaps today.

I've got terrible hay fever. I thought it was a cold or bug at first, but I had no temperature, so it was hay fever. I've got sore ears, nose, throat, and a sore on my arm, the last from karate.

I'm going to tell you what happened to me over the past days. Not necessarily in order.

I went to Shena's on Friday night to see the video 'E.T.' and a bit of 'Stand By Me' again. And I got a book with the story of 'Stand By Me' in it. It's called 'The Body – The Loss of Innocence' or something like that. I'll just have a look – Oh, the last part should be the 'Fall from Innocence', and it's by Stephen King.

I got to bed around 11:30 pm.

I went to Stages last night. The band was excellent. The singer was a real spunk. The drummer (I bumped into him and he said sorry) sounded really friendly. They are a different type of group. Not heavy metal, or anything. Sort of like the old Duran Duran, except with a girl in there. They sung all sorts of different songs ranging from Duran Duran to INX, and more. Heaps of people were there. Max Sutherland was with his mates. Stephen, one of them, Milly Newman's old boyfriend, recognised me and came and said hi. He's a nice guy.

I stayed with some flitterish 5th formers that I knew from school. They were probably flitterish because of the boys. There were those crazy 5th form guys there too, with

Alex Papadopolis. Spelt close enough like that. Well, it sounds the same. Or maybe it's Papadopolos. He used to like me when I was 14, but he was really short back then. Someone thought he looked like a girl at that age, but I didn't think so. Anyway, I got home after 11 pm.

I went to karate the next day. No Mike. I hurt my foot. Did something to my muscles in it as well as bruised it. It better get better before Tuesday's karate. I seem to be accident prone or something.

We did some fighting, which I liked, although in gradings it isn't as much fun, but I still enjoy it, probably because it feels sort of like playing. Well, not exactly, depends on who you get to fight. It wouldn't be playing for real. I can't describe in words what it feels like. I wonder what I would do if I have to fight Mike. I just don't know.

I can't be bothered saying any more – so I might talk later on. Especially about Mike. P.S. Danielle Nicholls may not be Mike's sister after all.

(Typed on a piece of paper)

I've got typing now, as you must have guessed already. I am in heaps of pain because my neck is all stuffed up and I can't move it much unless I want to get hurt more. All along the right side is so painful and stiff. I didn't want to go to school because of it. It must have come from sleeping funny. But it isn't a funny matter. I just wish it would go away. I've got P.E. next so I could rest upstairs and do nothing, or maybe I could read Shena's book.

It's mufti day today. It's a bit pointless for me because I wear mufti every day. Though, it's different when you see all the younger forms in mufti. Well, my younger sister's not complaining. The school is having it because they didn't get enough money from the last mufti day, so they can sponsor two kids' education.

Mike is here today. I don't know what to say next. In the rest of my diary you can guess what I wish. Well, anyway I still have this other wish; it's to go to the Olympics as a cyclist. I'm going to train in the summer, a lot!

I wish this neck ache would go away, it is real painful. I can't stand having it all day long. Not many people could anyway. I seem to be having a lot of trouble with soreness lately. I was aching on Thursday with a sore elbow; I think it was called tennis elbow even though I did it in karate. And I went and wacked my sore toe, the one that was dislocated, and on Sunday I did something during karate to my foot because I had to bandage it up when I got home. I could hardly walk on it, it was so painful. I think it could have been a cramp. And now this!

I've got to keep typing, since I have about 15 minutes left before the bell goes and I need to look busy. If there are spelling mistakes in here it's because I can't look at the typewriter properly due to my _____ neck. I better not swear or else someone will probably read this and I will get into trouble. They better not read it or they will be the ones who will be in trouble! I also forgot to put down that I had this great big whopping bruise under a blood vessel in my right hand, and I couldn't move my smaller fingers at the end properly, and it's still a bit there. I'm even getting a sore neck on the other side due to leaning on it, because of the _____ other side. I seem to be complaining a lot now, well, you can't exactly blame me for it with my bad luck lately with injuries.

Though, I wouldn't mind everything that's happening to me if I didn't have these aches and pains, and I would be in pure heaven if Mike asked me out. I really would.

I can't be bothered writing any more since the bell should go soon. I wish it would go now.

P.S. I want to know what mark I got for my art folio.

So far I'm pleased with my marks for school, and they are flukes. Pure flukes. So far I've passed all my subjects with Typing 50% (which was lucky due to that stuff up in one of my exams), Biology 51% (bye, bye, not doing you ever again), Art 63% and Computers 64%. But for Art I could get at least 68% because of the scaling that they will be doing. I got second in my class and first out of the Graphic Artists. English is the only mark I haven't got back yet. It's one of my best subjects. I may get it back in the last period, because all the other subjects gave their marks out today. Thinking about it, I might even get a 1 for Art, but I reckon it may take another one of my flukes, although since I came second in the class I should get it, since they give a 1 to the first three people with the highest mark. Though, I'm not sure whether it's all the classes put together or per class. Well, I hope it means one class each.

Bye for now.

SATURDAY
5
NOVEMBER

I went to a Campus Life dance last night and it had a small fireworks display and games to win an award, which was a mechanic suit with writing over it, like the one Vince Martin wears. Howick-Pakuranga won it, whereas my group came second. All the Campus Life clubs from South Auckland were there. The people from our club (even though this is the first time I've even been) were really nice. In the competition I hurt my dislocated toe, but it's OK now. Ours was the only other group in the circle besides Howick-Pakuranga's. To do the game, you had to stay in the circle without being pushed out until you were one of the last 3 people remaining. There were heaps of people there. The boys' competition was won by my group: 3 guys from our club.

Well, enough of talking about that. I must do some work around the house. Anyway, we got Guy Fawkes (fireworks) tonight. I'll talk to you a bit later.

SUNDAY
6
NOVEMBER

I guess I didn't write back yesterday, I didn't have the time.

I saw Mike at the fireworks display. He looked so gorgeous. He didn't go to karate today, though, neither did his friend Liam. But Mike will have to go next Sunday because it's the 5th kyus' (yellow belts) grading.

I'll be going to karate on Tuesday finally. I have to get my hours up since I missed heaps due to my dislocated toe.

Sorry about the mess the pen is making. It's leaking all over my hands and the paper. Probably because of the position it's in all the time. Downwards.

I should improve my writing in the book, I write too slack or in a hurry. Well, too bad anyway.

You know the notes that I have in this book that are separate? Well, I write them at school when I'm bored in class or have nothing else to do, but lately I've been reading instead. So far I have read one book and am part way through another. They are written by Stephen King, who is a really good writer. The first book that I read was called 'Different Seasons'. It was made up of separate stories – four altogether. It had 'Stand By Me' in it (called 'The Body' here). Now I'm reading 'Christine', which is about a haunted car. These books are close to 600 pages long. There's even one around 1000 pages, but I haven't read that one yet. I got the books from Shena. She's got a collection of them.

Back to talking about the karate gradings again. They said that only two yellow belts are going to be graded, because they have trained regularly. The others haven't done enough hours yet. I think I know who will be graded, since they go all the time. My grading will be here soon, and I'm going to make sure that I have enough hours of training to do it.

I better go and do some work now, I may be back to write later or if I don't I'll probably write when I get some time.

MONDAY
7
NOVEMBER

(But somehow feels like a Tuesday)

I'm fed up. I'm just fed up with boys. I just can't seem to get them out of my head. Or more likely I can't get one guy out of my head. I'm just sick and tired of thinking about him when I know I can't go out with him. And it makes me BLOODY angry, and I'm going to change all of this to fit what I want for once, and not dream for the impossible. I'll tell you about it in just a second after some jobs that I have to do or I'll get in trouble.

Back now. I'm not going to be a stupid idiot anymore. I'm not going to make a fool of myself anymore, and I'm going to have some time to myself and not think about boys! Because they piss me off. All I ever seem to do is make a fool of myself in front of them and I'm not going to do that again. I'm going to wise up to them now. I'm not going to be humiliated anymore. And I'm not going to look out for them anymore. And I mean it! If I don't keep my word I'll just get hurt more and I'll deserve it for being so naive. If guys aren't interested in me it's their own fault, not mine, it's them who'll be missing out, not me, and I don't really give a stuff now. I'm just going to get on with my own life, not theirs. If a boy asks me out, fine, that will be bloody great if I like him, but until then I'm just going to play it cool. I'm going to enjoy my summer without them ruining it and with them having me look childish and all mushy over them.

From now on I'm going to be myself, not someone acting stupid to impress a guy or following them around. They can piss off for all I care right now. I'm just so mad at them and their stupid games, which I will not take one second longer!!!!!!!!!!!!!!

TUESDAY
8
NOVEMBER

I must have rambled on for ages yesterday, probably just wanting to use up the empty space in this book, or it was more likely I was pissed off. Anyway, I'm perfectly fine today. I've read heaps of 'Christine' and I've got a 'Guns 'n' Roses' video tape from Shena.

On Thursday I've got my Bio trip, all day long.

I've got karate tonight at 6:30. I've only been once on a Tuesday, and that was before I dislocated my toe. Last time there was only me, a yellow belt and a blue belt, and we had a black belt each. I hope it will be good tonight. Last time we did fighting when I was there, and I had to fight all the black belts.

The back of my head is hurting now, right at the bottom, I don't know why, but I wish it would go away. Sorry, I broke my flow there, didn't I? I just say what comes into my head sometimes. I get told I go off in tangents (I think that's the word). I could be doing something, then I will say something else out of the blue, like when a serious bit is happening in a movie and I'll say loudly, "She's wearing a nice dress." I get a look from whoever else is watching, like: "She's dying and you're saying that?" But it probably was a really nice dress, so why not say it? My dad says things at important points like

69

that too, but intentionally. When someone is dying or has been shot in a TV programme, he'll say: "Don't worry, they'll get up and get paid", totally ruining the moment. Or sometimes he might say, "They'll get paid extra for that." He always has a smile on his face when he's saying it, and he always gets a loud "D-a-d!!!" in return.

Anyway, about tonight. I'm going to get 'Neighbours' taped and the first 10 minutes of 'V'. It's the final tonight. Should be good.

I hope that there will be some brown belts at karate, because last time there was only one and all he did was sit and watch. It should still be different. I think I want the brown belts there because they are my age and the highest you can go if you're under 18. I want to be that good someday.

I am so excited, because soon I won't have to go to school anymore. On Thursday it's the last day for classes and on Friday it's sign out day. I am just so excited that I can do what I always wanted now (after Friday morning). I have all the time in the world. I have about 2 and ½ months of holidays. It's that great!!! All the 7th and 5th formers have had their last day at school today, except for the exam and book return days, so it's going to be so quiet at school.

I want to buy the Fan Club album, because the song sung by them 'Paradise' is my favourite song at the moment. They have other really good songs too – 'Sensation' and 'Call Me.'

Today, Clara suggested joining a dance group and I think it's a good idea. Lauren (not my sister) wants to do the same.

I've got Computer Studies first tomorrow, while the computer test will be on Thursday. I've got Typing second and I've got to finish my project then – if I can. I'll have to do it at lunch time. 3rd period is P.E. Nothing wrong about that. It will be a lot quieter because there won't be any 5th formers. For 4th period I have English and I will hand my story over. No problem there. And last will be my final EVER Bio lesson. Yey!!!

On Thursday I have Art first, and I will do my mural then. I won't finish it on time – too bad – but I still enjoyed doing it. Second is the Computer test on file handling, which I will fail, but personally I don't care, and there's no way I'm doing Computers again. 3rd is Typing. I will probably do a Christmas card thing then, so it'll be a good period. And after that will be Study, which I will most likely dedicate to art. And last, but certainly not least, is my final subject for the whole year – English. It will be a good period because we're going to watch the 3 videos that our class filmed. My group filmed ours today. It was so funny, but I got a headache out of it. At least I missed Bio due to doing it, so it was worth it, headache and all.

I've read heaps of 'The Stand' but it will take a lot of time to finish because it has well over 700 pages. 734 to be exact. I want to read all the books that Stephen King has written, also I want to read a whole lot of other books as well – including Sara Collins, and the lady who wrote 'Lace'.

Well, I have plenty more to write, but 'North and South', the new miniseries, has just started and I want to watch it, so I'll write the rest tomorrow.

Bye!!!

Sorry I didn't write when I said I would. Anyway, I bought the Fan Club album – it's good. And the best thing of all – School is finished! I won't be going back for approximately two and a half months. Isn't that great?

I went to karate today. Only one black belt showed up, the oldest one. We did heaps of things. I've got to check whether they are marking me off the roll or not, because sometimes they don't call my name out. What a bummer. I'll be going on Tuesday, so I can check then.

The 5th form exams start tomorrow – not counting their music exam on Friday. Thank goodness I don't have to do anymore exams or stuff for school.

This school year went so quick – it's unbelievable. I think it's a leap year. I'm not sure. But that's only one day.

I'm going to do heaps of things in the holidays. It'll be so excellent. I've already read three books by Stephen King that Shena gave me, and I've got one more at home to read. Also, I'm going to go to the library and get all sorts of other books out. And, I'm going to do a lot of artwork, mainly dealing with sculptures and stuff like that, and I'll make clothes and design my own too.

I want to train; the only problem is getting off my butt and doing it, not just talking about it. I should set up a sort of timetable, even though I may not do it like that, it still could give me other ideas that are similar. I can try and do it from tomorrow.

There's swimming,

running,

cycling,

weights,

and there is also that rowing machine Dad has.

My brother used to have these things that went around the ankles with weights. He would run with them on. I could use something like that. Also, I need more sleep. I stayed up too late reading. I don't want bags under my eyes, now do I.

On a different note, I'm going to watch heaps of videos in the holidays. There are loads that I want to see. I reckon the holidays are going to be good for me. And also, I won't be going out of my mind over those boys, because I won't be seeing them much. Maybe they will be going to karate, but I won't have to look at them every day. Good!

I love holidays, they are so excellent, especially because you don't have the pressure of school with homework and other stuff. I can do whatever I want now, so I won't ever be bored like in school.

I'm glad I bought The Fan Club album – it's really good, I'm listening to it now.

Well, I better go help Mum with the birds.

At Night

Tomorrow I'm going down the road so I can do shopping with Mum and Clara, then we'll get a video out to watch. I also want to go to the library, just wish I could spend ages there.

Miss World was on tonight. Miss Iceland won. Let's hope that I will start training tomorrow. The problem with me is that I'm lazy in the morning – I just can't be blowed to get up for a run. Well, most people are like that, but I won't be able to get anywhere with sport if I just laze in bed and not train. Other athletes can do it, so I must try my best.

Goodnight!

Went to see Aunty Tiana's new house yesterday for her birthday. It was gorgeous inside – the lounge was so beautiful and it had gorgeous paintings.

I finished reading 'Lace' today. It's different from the miniseries on TV. Two of the women from the book were combined into one for the miniseries.

My younger sister went to hospital today to get her foot fixed up. She left home around 10 in the morning and came back just after 8 at night.

Last Friday I went to Shena's and watched a video and played her video game.

I've got karate tomorrow and another of the white belts that is a friend said she will go too for the first time on a Tuesday. Her name's Melanie or Celia. I don't know. I get her sister's and her name mixed up. I think it is Melanie. Yep, I'm pretty definite it's Melanie – I think? Actually, I'm not sure??

I reckon the holidays are great. And also I'm not crazy over Mike anymore. Most likely because I haven't seen him since I finished school. Although, when I do see him I'll probably get all stupid again. Still, it's pretty good not being high-strung over a guy. High-strung really isn't the right word for it, but close: girlish, babyish, whatever. I reckon the word 'crush' really does describe how you feel when you fall for someone, because it crushes you, or more accurately – your heart, especially if they don't return your feelings.

I've got nothing else to say – So Goodnight.

WEDNESDAY
30
NOVEMBER

It's the last day of November for this year and in 25 days it'll be Christmas day.

I was right, the girl from karate was Melanie and her sister was Celia. Celia has a crush on Liam, who is going out with Vicky. Celia lives next door to him. I don't blame her for being jealous. Man, she must be pissed off, although Vicky is a really nice person, friendly anyway.

I went with Mum and my younger sister to Mum's exercises the other day. She came second for her hat (a fun) competition and her friend came first. My sister won a raffle that Mum gave her a ticket for. We then went shopping, etc. It was a good day.

Got karate tomorrow, and on Friday Shena is coming over. I've got to get a good video. I don't know what she has seen. I saw 'Moving Target' last Saturday with my younger sister. It was good.

I've been collecting a lot of recipes today so I can do some cooking in the holidays. I've got heaps of them out of the old Woman's Day magazines that Mum gave me. I've finished all of my library books, except for one. I think I might try to finish it by Friday so I can take it back when I get the video.

I want to start doing up my room now, because I said some time ago that I wanted to rearrange it, but I didn't have the time back then. Well, I certainly have the time now, and I want to (maybe) do some of my own furniture and other things, like making some clothes and writing a book. Actually, more than one book, but I think it would be best to concentrate on one at a time. I get ahead of myself sometimes.

Yesterday at karate we went over a grading for practice. It felt like a drill. The two sisters were there so I didn't have to do the exercises alone. Phew! My grading will probably be this Sunday or the next one. At last! I'll be going for the 7th kyu. It's the belt with two red stripes on it. I reckon the best way to approach karate is to work for the grade that is one ahead, because it's no use setting your sights on a black belt when you're still only a white belt and have at least 5 years of training to get there. It's stupid doing that and you will soon get pretty bored waiting for it, so the best thing is to set your sights on the grade in front of you and then climb to success. Karate's so neat; I don't think I will ever get bored of it. Well, so far that's obvious because I go to all the training sessions they have – Sunday, Tuesday, and Thursday.

I've got to remember to say 'White Rabbit' tomorrow morning – before I speak to anyone else. It's supposed to be good luck. I'm not superstitious or anything, I just think it's fun.

White Rabbit.

I did remember to say 'White Rabbit' first thing on Thursday. I just thought I should write that. At least I remembered.

I've got this aching back, on the shoulder part. It's really sore. It's on my left side. I woke up and went to itch my back and I pulled a muscle. What a bummer. It isn't quite as bad as when I'd done my neck in though. That was really bad and sore.

I went to town with Mum yesterday, got Christmas presents and a record by King for me, the last only $2. Good aye? Mum and I had lunch at Farmers (the big department store in town) and we got home around 2 or just before. It was a good day.

Clara phoned me to go over to her place for a barbecue with some others, but I was too tired and I had to tidy up some stuff.

I went to karate, and again I went over my grading. I wonder when I'm going to go over it for real.

Last Friday, I went to a party at a person's place from the Methodist church. I went with Amy and Lauren, and got a free lift there.

On Saturday, I went to the beach with Mum and my younger sister after I had done the lawn, and I met Amy and the others from the party and church, while Mum and my sister went to another part of the beach. Anyway, this old guy creeped me out, actually, he might not have been that old, possibly in his twenties. I don't think he was with the group, just butted in. Still, he definitely creeped me out because he was asking me questions, and I think he wanted me to go with him. No way! I excused myself and avoided him after that. I eventually went home with my friends Lauren and Amy. Boy, can they be a pain sometimes. They took so much time to leave.

I went to karate on Sunday, same as usual. Amy came and it looked like she wanted to join in, but she turned up late, so she just sat and watched until she had to leave.

What a mess my writing is. It's partly because of my sore back and anyway, I keep making mistakes and I'm writing fast. So next time I will try to print neatly. Usually at school, I write in the joining technique.

(What a mess)

FRIDAY
9
DECEMBER

I didn't go to karate yesterday because of my sore back, shoulders, and neck. I wonder who was there? Probably the same people. I've got to ring Amy so she will be able to join. I saw her the other day walking past my house (across the street) with this guy. She had some flowers and was talking ninety-miles an hour. I thought it was funny and one of the Murphys who was riding past did too. (Well, it looked like he was smiling). I wonder who her new boyfriend is. She gets them so easily.

My neck is really good right now, the soreness will probably be totally gone by tomorrow. I went to Shena's today, and saw a video called 'Vice Versa', which was about a father and son swapping bodies. It was really funny. I also fixed my tape (the Bon Jovi one) that my younger sister taped some songs over. Shena gave me a couple of videos to take home to watch. I had lunch there.

Mum and I went shopping in Panmure. Didn't buy clothes there, but I got my brother a Christmas present, which was some really nice mug glasses at an excellent price.

I couldn't find the togs I wanted at Panmure, so Mum and I went to Pakuranga and I got one from the boutique store. It's really nice, it was either that one or a blue and white one, but I chose the pink and white one, because I like pink better. I'm not really a fan of blue.

When I got home, I had dinner and watched 'Secret Admirer'. I'd seen it before, but it's really good so I got the video off Shena. Man, would I ever love to have a guy like that. You know, be buddy friends with a guy then end up going out with him. I've always wished that some really nice guy would move in next door and that we could be real good friends.

I've got to write a whole lot of letters to pen pals that I want to have. I'll probably start that tomorrow. Also, I got my first Christmas card from Jill, so I've got to start sending out some of my own. I wonder whether I will get one from a boy. I guess it's too much to ask for.

I'll be going to karate on Sunday. I hope that the grading isn't then, but next week, because I was away on Thursday and I won't know what's happening.

Tomorrow, I will probably be going for a ride to the shops to do something for Mum, I don't know yet, probably for some groceries or letters.

I need to wash my hair tomorrow too, because it's such a mess. My skin's getting really greasy on my face now, so I have to dry it out with that Clearskin stuff.

I'm reading 'The Neverending Story' at the moment, because I've finished all my library books. It's quite good. The book I was reading before that was by Victoria Holt and it was called 'Shimmering Sands' and it was good too. It had such an unexpected finish – about the murderer. But it ended happily for the main characters and she got the guy that I reckon was the best. I really love to read, it's like a hobby or even more than that.

I'm not so sure about being a lawyer now. It was something that I became interested in after watching 'L.A. Law'. I love to write so I think I could be a writer. I also love art so I could also become a graphic artist. I don't know.

Next year I'm taking:

1) Art   )

2) Art – Sculpture   > Graphic Artist

3) Art History   )

4) History   )

                         > Writing or a lawyer (the second
                            career I don't think so anymore)
5) English   )

I love History so I think that it would be perfect to take, also it would be good to take if I want to be a writer. And, I could work as a graphic artist and write in my spare time, and design covers for books. I reckon that's a great idea. Also, I reckon my next year will decide what I'll do the following year: whether it's going to university or tech.

I hope I do well next year. You need to in Bursary, especially if you want to go to university or tech. I don't know what to do if I don't get into either of them.

I reckon the best time to write is at night when it's all quiet and dark except for the desk light. You can concentrate more and come up with some interesting stories. A dream is a story. But they're pretty weird ones, because the people are always changing in them and you are often in one place then the next. They are definitely weird.

The days are going really quickly now. I hope that school doesn't come back too soon. I've only just finished it. So far we've had about 3 weeks off school, which I think is fantastic.

Well, I better go to bed now; it's getting a bit too late. 10:55 pm to be exact.

Goodnight.

I hope I get more Christmas cards. I've also got to send some, and if I post them down the road I can get more library books out.

I've just got two presents left to get – Dad's and Clara's. I know what I'm getting Dad – some socks, but I don't know what to give Clara.

I've got to wrap up some of my presents today. I wonder where we will be having Christmas this year; you know, when all our relations gather together. My older sister and brother will probably come and see us in the afternoon, and we will go wherever the big gathering is. My neighbour and his friend will probably come over for lunch or around that time.

I've got to do something to my room. Glitz it up, or something else to make it look interesting.

I can't wait to we get our Christmas tree. I like to decorate it and they always look beautiful.

My younger sister will be finishing school this Tuesday so we can get videos out. Soon all schools will be out – even the little primary kids.

I better go and do some work now – so bye.

Continued – Saturday

Went to the Yugoslav club tonight. Some people dressed up because it was a masquerade dance. Got karate tomorrow. I might also be doing the lawn. I haven't started writing to those pen pals yet. It will be neat having a whole lot of people writing to me. They have different pen pals each week (I think) on the Teletext. I want to send in my name so it's put on TV, so that someone will write to me.

I'm going to go to work with Dad on Tuesday and tidy up his work place. I wish I had a part-time job somewhere close to home.

I'm going to do some sunbathing in my new togs soon – maybe tomorrow. Clara will be away all this week, so I could invite Shena over or Amy or even go and see her new place.

Well, I better get some sleep.

Goodnight.

SUNDAY
11
DECEMBER

I went to karate. It was very hard at the beginning – mainly because of the press ups, 100 of them altogether. You should see my knuckles, they're sore as, because we don't do normal press ups on the flat of our hands; we do them on the two biggest knuckles. You close your hands like a fist, then place your two biggest knuckles from each hand on the ground and press up from them. It doesn't matter whether it's on the concrete outside or on the hard wood inside, we still do them, but luckily we did them inside today, plus it would be mean to make us do 100 knuckle press ups on the concrete.

I also practiced what I will be doing in my grading, because I found out that I have it for real on Thursday. We did sparring during the session too; I was involved with fighting a person who was being graded. I only had to do it once.

After karate, there was a barbecue at one of the black belt's house, Lucas – I think that's his name.

I watched 'The Return of Sherlock Holmes' tonight. It was rather good. Watergate was mentioned in it. I want to know what it is and what happened. Watergate? I must look it up.

Anyway, I wrapped all of my presents for Christmas and Mum's one looks neat with the ribbons and all. I even fixed up a little gift tab with it. It looks excellent. I must make the other gifts look good too. I've still got to get Clara's and Dad's presents, and also send a couple of cards off. And I can't forget to write to my pen pals. Maybe I can send a card off to the New Zealander or even to the Japanese ones as well. I'm also definitely going to send my name into Teletext so more people can write to me. It would be great to have a lot of pen pals.

I want to get some Sherlock Holmes books. And I must ring Amy to tell her about karate. I hope my knuckles get better. And I should also try and find Melanie's phone number. She lives next door to Liam Hudsworth. Celia, her sister, has a crush on him.

I'm going to go to work with Dad on Tuesday, and on Wednesday I might be doing next door's lawn.

I better go to bed now.

Laku noć

(Goodnight in Yugoslav)

SUNDAY
18
DECEMBER

I went to one of my friend's birthday party. It was excellent. We went to the beach first. My new togs were excellent. I went windsurfing for the first time. Well, I had a try.

It was my last karate lesson for the year yesterday and I got my certificate for my grade, which was cool. I didn't go for the barbecue. Mum, my younger sister, and I went shopping today at Panmure. I posted my Christmas cards.

WEDNESDAY
21
DECEMBER

I have just finished reading 'The Godfather' by Mario Puzo. It was amazing. I must look the mafia up and also Watergate.

I got the book 'Savages'. Mum brought it home yesterday.

I saw a real cute guy today. He's a milk boy. I've seen him before, but was not interested. But today he was so cute and I love it when guys wear cut-off shirts and they have muscly arms. I have to see him some more, I just have to check what days he does his milk run on.

Also, I want to start up jogging, but I always seem to put it off. What a bummer. I must get fitter. I'm getting a bit too heavy. My weight is alright, but I mean the way I look. I don't want to be flabby.

I need to make a lot of friends next year, even if I don't sit with them. I must be really friendly. It's my last year at high school and it's going to be my best.

I've got 4 Christmas cards left. One for Clara and I'll decide what to do with the rest later. I'll probably be going to the shops tomorrow. I must get Clara's present as well. Also, I can take back some library books.

I went to Shena's house today, saw 'Some Kind of Wonderful'. I'm going to get Poison's tape from her, which she will get from Diana. I also must remember to ring Clara.

I've been writing heaps of letters lately. I wrote 4 on Sunday – Christmas day – and one very long one today. I don't know why, but I can't seem to stop writing them. I had a real gala day writing my last one. I wrote 4 and a half pages. I just want people to write to me, I don't mind what they say just as long as they write.

I finished reading 'Savages' by Shirley Conran last night. It was absolutely brilliant. It's one of the best that I have ever read. 'The Outsiders' and 'Savages' are the best books. Also 'The Godfather' was brilliant and 'The Poseidon Adventure' was very well written.

I got a new diary for Christmas from my older sister. It's a real nice one. So on the first of January I will start writing in that book instead of here.

That cute milk boy does work on – oh, I forgot – well, too bad. Maybe it was ... oh, I don't know.

New Year's Day is this Sunday – the week after Christmas. I'm going to see the film 'Big' – maybe tonight?

I want to be a writer. Why else do I love reading and coming up with all these ideas for stories. I'm going to work on this one which I like a lot – the idea, that is. It's going to be about this girl and boy. The boy is part Puerto Rican and

American, he's 17-years-old and is in his last year at high school. He's a brilliant artist and poet, but hides it because he's shy about his work. He starts having trouble at home when his Puerto Rican mother, who is grateful to her husband for pulling her out of the Bronx, begins drinking heavily after finding out that he plays around. The father knows that the mother will never leave since she will own nothing without him, but he's tired of her, which is why he has affairs, and when she drinks he loses his temper and slaps her around. The boy is over protective of his mother and is constantly fighting with his father. They live in a middle class place so they aren't poor, but the boy soon joins up with a gang of the poorer kids since he can't stand being around the richer ones, because they remind him of his father. He is in constant trouble at school and gets in fights with the richer guys. He dresses like the poorer kids and sometimes he runs away from home after he has a fight with his father. He always goes to the same place – a beautiful spot by a stream. This is where he is able to concentrate and draw and do poems. It's one place he is able to be by himself.

He has a little sister aged 6, and a little brother aged 12. He loves his sister dearly and is afraid that she will get hurt during the fighting.

The main girl in the story is from England and moves to America with her father and mother. She starts going to the boy's high school. She has blonde hair, cut to just above the shoulders in a Cleopatra style, except all the one length. Her father is a well-known English architect, who becomes the president of the number one architecture business in America, which is why they moved there. The mother is an old English starlet, who was a hit back in the early 60s and late 50s as an actress and is considering returning to acting, this time in America.

The girl can be called Shelley or Cassandra, while the boy will be called Mike, I think. Well, the girl becomes popular instantly and all the boys start asking her out, but she chooses the lead football player, who is handsome and the most popular boy, but is very vain. Even though all the guys like her, Mike doesn't. He reckons she's a stuck-up rich bitch, and ignores her or causes trouble. He reckons she is just like all the rich kids who remind him of his father.

Well, anyway, she is in his Art, English, and Liberal Studies classes.

She also avoids Mike, because of his reputation, but is still fascinated with the way he acts, even though she is scared of him. Mike, who is extremely handsome with a dark complexion, high cheekbones, and a fine nose and black eyes, is in turn the talk of all the girls at school. Because of this, the rich girls frequently dare each other to hit on him, even though they know he doesn't like them. He will only go out with the poorer ones.

In Liberal Studies, a marriage project is happening, so the teacher pairs couples up. Cassandra's boyfriend is in the class too. When the teacher pairs Mike and Cassandra, Mike gets hassled by her boyfriend and told not to do anything to her or else. However, Cassandra is slowly growing sick of her boyfriend – his name is Robert or Stewart – and starts having feelings for Mike, but she acts as if she doesn't like him, because she is scared of what her boyfriend might do if she became entangled with Mike.

Mike doesn't like her, but slowly stops being hostile towards her and eventually falls for her. When they do finally get together and confess their feelings for each other, everyone tries to break them apart, but they fight back and stay together.

Their song will be 'A Town Without Pity' and that will be the name of the book.

Name Ideas:

Boy – Mike, Matt.

Girl – Amanda, Cassandra, Danielle, or Donna could be good names for her, also Sandra, Sarah, Shelley.

THURSDAY
29
DECEMBER

I went to see 'Big' last night with my younger sister and one of my cousins. The film was so sweet.

I got all my pen pal letters posted yesterday.

Soon it will be New Year's Eve, then New Year's Day. 1989 will be here on Sunday. I'm not sure what we will be doing exactly on New Year's Eve – might be at the Yugoslav Club. I love going to the Yugoslav picnic, but I'm not that interested in going to the club.

―――――――――――

I wonder if I'll get any letters from the pen pals I sent away for. I reckon my best letter was to that guy from Dunedin. It must be lovely down there. I would love to go and see the South Island. They had a programme about it tonight with Leeza Gibbons in it. Beautiful scenery and places.

Well, I better get some sleep now – so goodnight.

Laku noć

FRIDAY
30
DECEMBER

I wonder what school will be like in "89". There won't be any of this year's 7th form there, so that means Clara's boyfriend Mike (not my Mike) and also Lauren (not my sister) will be gone. And a lot of this year's 6th form won't be coming back either.

We will be going on a camp next year for school. I hope we go to Motitapu - I think you spell it that way. I'll just check. Nope, it was Motatapu. I've never been there before.

Also, I hope I do well in "89". I need to do good at school, because it's the bursary year.

I hope I get some letters from my pen pals. I like writing, it's neat.

———————————

Things I would like to do or happen in the year "89"

1) Do extremely well in my subjects at school.
2) Join the school committees and be one of the leaders, especially in the social committee.
3) Go to the school ball (with a spunky guy).
4) Go out with a guy, someone who I really like.

5) Do extremely, extremely well in karate.

6) Do extremely well at school for sports and at all competitions in sport.

7) Become very popular.

8) Be a liaison officer.

9) Have a lot of pen pals.

10) Get a job – a good one. Part-time – hopefully at Denny's.

11) Write a book, a big one – a novel.

Things that I can do to be popular

1) Join committees, clubs, etc.

2) Help people – be friendly.

3) Always smile and say hi to people.

4) Talk to people I know and don't know.

5) If anyone is by themselves, talk to them – whether they're 3rd or 7th formers – remember you were like them once – do unto others what you wish them to do unto you.

6) Don't be shy.

7) Don't just talk to girls, talk to guys. Let them know what you're really like. Offer to help them with their homework.

8) Also, I must dress good, be clean, and smell good. Use my

nice smelling soaps for my baths or showers, put nice perfume on, shave my legs perfect, put nice smelling moisturiser on them, wash underarm every morning and put roll-on and powder on. Have clean nails – both toes and fingers. Take spray and makeup with me to school. Have clean, nice smelling clothes. Wear clothes for the occasion, not hot stuff on a boiling day so I won't stink. Put powder in my shoes so they don't stink. Always have sparkling teeth and good breath. Buy breath cleanser – or something like that. Don't wear too much jewellery or makeup, have just the right amount on. Walk, talk, and hold head up high. Be confident. Always have a watch. Always wash around the neck and ears and in ears. Have a good wash in the morning. Have hair clean and done beautifully. Curl it with curling comb and wash it with nice smelling shampoo and conditioner. Have split ends cut off. Talk properly. Don't mumble. Smile and be happy – try to cheer up anyone who is down.

9) Be responsible with people, don't argue, don't lose your cool.

10) Be charming, compliment people, charm them.

11) <u>Don't</u> tell lies. They can hurt and make you feel guilty. Don't be guilty, because if you don't do anything wrong, your conscience will be free.

12) Don't swoon over boys. If you like them, get to know them and be friendly – Say hi or something, talk to them,

because if you don't it's no use being stupid and going goo goo over them. Don't let boys look down at you. Be proud of yourself, but not stuffy. Don't be vain. Don't be bullied – stand up to the culprits. Talk reason. Don't complain no matter what. Don't be a whinger.

13) Smile.

—————————

I must make the most of my holidays, and not just let them pass me by. I must also make the most of what I've got. I should be more grateful, especially to my parents. I should do more things – I shouldn't have to be told to tidy things up. I need to make everyone happy – at home as well as at school, everywhere. Sometimes I trim the edges of the lawn without being asked, I think my parents like me doing that, and it keeps me busy. I must always be busy, I don't know why, I get hyperactive sometimes. I suppose it's why I exercise so much. I need to be doing things all the time, my mind races ahead of my body. It's sort of like I'm aching to jump out of my skin, because I'm not moving fast enough. It's hard to explain.

SATURDAY
31
DECEMBER

New Year's Eve.

We're going to the Yugoslav Club tonight. I'm going to tidy up my room now, so I'll write later.

I need to lose weight on my legs and stomach (waist), and I should learn to swim better, so I'll go to the pools to train. I need to know how to dive better as well.

I must make time for training – be determined to learn and become fitter and better. Also, I must take better care of my hands, in particular my fingernails, because I bite them. It's a nervous reaction to almost anything; I do it even when I'm bored. Actually, that's when I do it the most.

Diary 1989

MONDAY
2
JANUARY

Saturday night, Dad, Mum, Nina, and I went to the Yugoslav club. We stayed there to just past 12:30 pm.

Sunday morning, Mum, Nina, and I went to church. When we got home, Dad joined us and we went to say 'Happy New Year' to our neighbours. I think we got back just before one o'clock. Later on we went to Aunty Vesna's place. We stayed there till about 9:45 pm.

Lena, a girl from the club and also a relation, I think from Uncle Luka's side, was there. Well, anyway, she reckons the girls snob her too, and that she gets bored like me, so next time I go to the club I'll have someone to talk to.

I did some more jogging. I went this morning and at 8:00 at night. The morning run was around 11:30, so it was boiling hot and I couldn't do much more than half an hour. The night run was for 40 minutes. It went well until I got a heat rash on my legs and it started to burn. It was very painful. I also went for a swim at the local pool. It was only a short one because they had to close.

I'm going to Rainbow's End tomorrow from 9:30 to around 6 at night with my younger sister and the boy next door. The boy's mother is taking us.

I'm going to see Torvill and Dean this Saturday with Mum at the Big Top, which is at the Epsom Grounds. It's going to be excellent. Also, there will be Russian ice skaters too, who will do excellent Russian dances on the ice.

TUESDAY
3
JANUARY

We didn't go to Rainbow's End today, because of the weather, so we'll go tomorrow at the same time. I went running instead, this time in the late afternoon. Due to the heat rash, I wore my cycling pants. It was much better than wearing the other shorts, because they didn't rub.

My younger sister, her friend, and I got two videos out. It only cost five dollars for both. We saw 'Teen Wolf Too' and the 'American Nynga' (I don't know how to spell the second word). Anyway, they were both good and the second one was excellent. 'Ninja' – that's how you spell it, Mum just told me.

Shena just rang. I invited her to go to Rainbow's End tomorrow. She couldn't go today because she went to Piha then Orewa, somewhere in that direction anyway. She said it was nice and sunny up there. So, now at least I will have someone to talk to, because my sister will go off with her friend.

The holidays are going very fast, I reckon. Already I've had practically two months of holidays. Soon I will be a big 7th former. Well, the 3rd formers look at the 7th formers like they are adults. I remember when I was in the 3rd form the 7th formers looked so big and mature, only now do I look at those 7th form boys as immature.

I feel like writing some more letters, only I haven't got any replies from the other ones that I've written to. That's probably because of all the public holidays. Hopefully, some will come tomorrow. But, I will have to wait till just after six to see whether I have any since I will be at Rainbow's End practically all day.

Karate starts again soon - on the 12th, next Thursday. I hope I become really good at karate. The boy from next door, my sister's friend, was a yellow belt in Taekwondo and his father was a brown belt.

I've got to draft the badminton skirt pattern sometime before badminton starts again. I wonder when it will be starting. I also wonder whether Caleb will be there, because if he is it'll be mighty embarrassing, since I haven't seen or heard from him at all, not even after I gave a present to his sisters to give him for his birthday. Maybe he didn't like it. So be it, can't change things now.

SATURDAY
7
JANUARY

I finally got a letter from the first pen pal that I sent off for. Her name is Rachel Linton, and she is from Napier. I got it yesterday. She's in the 5th form this year and is fifteen.

I started a drawing of my Aunty Vesna and Uncle Luka in pencil.

I've started dieting yesterday. I'm using Victoria Principal's one week dieting program.

I have a cold so I don't think I'll be going to Piha tomorrow with Shena.

One of my cousins is coming over to stay the night, actually two nights.

Mum and I are going to see Torvill and Dean and the Russian Ice Skaters today. My cousin saw the show and she said it was excellent and that we will enjoy it. We have to get dressed up pretty snug because it's going to be cold there.

When the RTR Countdown magazine comes out I'm going to look in the pen pals column to see whether my name is in it. I hope it is. It may not be in this month's edition because of all the people that must be sending in, but I hope it will get in eventually.

THURSDAY
12
JANUARY

Karate starts back up tonight. At least I can get some more exercise. I've lost about 3 kilos this week from my diet.

I've got a new sun frock from a store in Takapuna. It can be used for school, the Yugoslav club, and other places. Mum paid for it. I bought some hair removing cream too. It will be much better than having to shave my legs.

I'll be missing karate on Sunday because I'll be going to Piha with Shena and her family. I'm going to invite her to the Yugoslav picnic.

I saw another 'American Ninja' film yesterday. I also saw 'The Pick-up Artist' with Shena.

I've written a gigantic letter to my pen pal from Napier. I used seven pages. I sent it off today. I hope I will get a boy pen pal too. I want to have as many as I possibly can.

I've finished reading 'The Scarlet Pimpernel'. The ending was different from the film as well as other things. I've still got three other books to read, not counting the one I'm reading now.

We seek him here,
We seek him there,
Those Frenchies seek him everywhere.

Is he in Heaven?
Is he in Hell?
That damned elusive Pimpernel.

That's the poem in the book. I reckon it's quite neat. The Scarlet Pimpernel said it in the book and movie himself.

The book was by Baroness Orczy.

I've been doing Aerobics OZ Style all this week. I haven't missed it once yet.

Torvill and Dean and the Russians were great on Saturday. The Russian guys were cute, especially one of them. I've taken heaps of pictures, but some were wasted and the flash didn't work a couple of times. The costumes were excellent, especially in the Egyptian segment and I also liked the hat dance and the card one because it was funny. The Egyptian one was sad though. But, all the performances were brilliant, quite dazzling.

School starts on the 31st for me, which is on a Tuesday. I wonder what class I will be in and who will be in it with me? The holidays are going so quick now. I can't wait for the Yugoslav picnic, that's always great. I bet it's on the Sunday before school starts up again for everyone, the 29th.

When this week has finished, I will only have two more weeks of my holidays left. Man, has it gone that fast? Soon I will be back into that daily routine of getting up on time for school. At first it may be alright, but once you have been lumped with homework again you've had it. But, one good thing about it is my subjects. I've taken two Art subjects, so I won't have to study for them. I've also taken History and English. History will be different; I've never taken it before. I hope we get a good subject, like the red Indians. And last but not least – English. That will be a good subject too, I hope. I also hope I will get good teachers. At least I know I will get good ones for the art subjects.

I hope this year will be great! And I'm definitely going to the ball. I'll probably be helping with it because I intend on being in the Social Committee, and also I intend on being in all the committees, including the Art's one. So, it looks like I am going to be real busy this year. Also, I intend on becoming popular, because I know this is my year.

SATURDAY
14
JANUARY

Clara came over yesterday and all of us (my family) went to the beach, except it rained so we came home.

Since it's practically only two weeks till school starts (the classes, not the pre-stuff), I'm going to make the most of my last days of freedom.

<u>What can I do in two weeks to fill up my time?</u>

1) Tennis – I can go down to the domain and play against the wall or go with Clara.

2) Zoo – Go for a one day trip. It'll be nice and I can take photos.

3) The pools – Go with Clara, my younger sister, or anybody for a swim.

4) Pictures – Go with Nina to see 'Who Framed Roger Rabbit'.

5) Squash – By myself or with anyone.

6) Bike Rides – Map out a route with Clara.

7) Beach – Go anytime – bike down with Clara or Nina.

8) Videos – Watch videos with Shena.

9) Badminton – Anywhere.

Got the Yugoslav picnic on the 29th. I'm going to invite Clara and Shena to come. Actually, I've already invited Clara.

SUNDAY
15
JANUARY

Mum, my younger sister and I went to church at 9:00 am, but we found out the time had been changed to 9:30, so while we waited we looked at the new video shop, and Mum got a membership card.

Shena and her family picked me up just before 11:00 and we drove out to Piha. It was raining, so we waited in the car for it to stop and had our lunch in there. After a little while, it cleared up enough to let us go on the beach. We walked in the water. Piha has huge waves and when you stand still in the sand and water, big rips come under your feet and pull the sand away. And when you look at your feet it looks like you're moving very fast.

We drew some names on the beach and sunbathed. Shena and I kept jumping the waves and getting our shorts wet. It was an excellent day out. I think I got home at 4:30 pm.

My younger sister and her friend, along with Shena and I are going to see 'Who Framed Roger Rabbit?' tomorrow, but before that I'm going to help Mum with the shopping. Mum is going to drop all of us off after the shopping is finished in time for the one o'clock session. We've got two free tickets for it: one for me and one for my sister. Mum won them. Since the tickets are so dear we're going to use the tickets for me and

Shena, and my sister and her friend will buy child tickets, so Shena will pay for my sister's ticket, which is $3.50 instead of paying an adult's ticket, which is $7.00, and a rip off, so everything will work out fine.

MONDAY
16
JANUARY

We saw 'Who Framed Roger Rabbit?' but my sister's friend didn't end up coming. Mum, my sister, and I went to pick up Shena and dropped my bike off to be fixed. Mum then went and did the shopping, and Shena and I went to look at some other shops, while my sister went her own way. I bought some postcards. I'm going to write on one and send it to my cousin Marina in Yugoslavia.

I've been reading the book 'The Queen's Confession' a lot and I only have about a hundred pages left. It's taking ages to read. It's about Marie Antoinette.

THURSDAY
19
JANUARY

I finally got down to 59 kilos, I'm no longer in the 60s'. Obviously. I'm real happy about losing weight. It makes me feel heaps better. I intend on shaping my body better and keeping myself fit. I've been doing aerobics every day for more than a week and I think it's showing. Also, I've cut down on food and am watching my diet, so I won't go back to 64 kilos again. I intend on getting to the middle 50s'.

Went to karate. It was boring, not like Tuesday. Tuesday was excellent because they let us fight, which was fun. Amy didn't go to karate tonight because she was on a trip. I hope the next karate session will be more interesting. I've got a bruise on a bruise now. I seem to collect them like postcards.

I'm going to the beach tomorrow. Hope it will be sunny. Mum, my younger sister, and I are going, and I might invite either Shena or Clara.

When I went to the library on Tuesday, I got 'Lace 2' out along with two other books. Well, I've finished two of the books so far, which means I only have four of them left. You might say I can't subtract, ha, ha, I have more at home. Obviously.

I wonder when I'm going to start badminton again. I'll just have to wait for the Times to come out. The Public Notices will have the date for when it starts back up again.

School is getting closer and closer, so I better learn my road code before there's no time to spare for it. 10 more days to school. I must get a tan. I've hardly been out in the sun much. Well, there's the Yugoslav picnic two days before school, so that will give me something, and plus tomorrow at the beach. Also, instead of reading inside on a hot day I'll sunbathe and read at the same time.

I must go to Shanton or the shop next to it before school, because I'll need a short skirt for the summer period. It's going to be boiling in February.

SUNDAY
22
JANUARY

At karate we had a real tough training session. We had to do kartas with different kicks, and that was very tiring. We also had to do fighting – that was fun. And, we were made to do 200 press-ups, that was NOT fun.

My name was on Teletex under the new members, but it's not yet on the pen pal's list. I've written a new pen pal down from the new list.

This week is going to be busy. Tomorrow we'll probably be going to Panmure or somewhere, and be doing work around the house. Tuesday, I'm going to find something to do that's easy. Wednesday is being spent with Mum and my younger sister – probably at the beach and Manukau. Thursday is to myself. Friday is at Shena's for videos. Saturday – all sorts. Sunday, the Yugoslav picnic.

I can't wait until the Yugoslav picnic. It's always excellent. I just pray it'll be fine weather, because the beach is fantastic. Shena's coming and I must see whether Clara is too. I've got to ring Clara and see how her trip went, plus I want to talk to her about what we can do for our last week before school starts up again.

Also, I must ring up Denny's for a job interview. And, sooner or later I must learn my road code book. I've got to ask Clara what part of the book I should learn.

MONDAY
23
JANUARY

I will get a boyfriend this year. I'm sure of it. But I wish these New Zealand blokes weren't so shy. I wish they were more like the guys in Yugoslavia, who were more forward, like when I went there just before my 16th birthday. They chased us there. There were some really nice guys, but unfortunately there were also a couple of idiots as well. I learned to say 'na pusti me', which I said when I wanted them to leave me alone, because those two wouldn't stop bugging me and my younger sister. Idiots. I liked two others though; I danced with one of them at a party. Those two were both gorgeous. I say gorgeous a lot, but when a boy is, what else is there to use? I suppose handsome, but that sounds like what an old person would say.

I wonder who is staying at school this year. Quite a lot of people are leaving. Some of them are Jill Rainey, Hannah Doran, Andrea Smith and so on. I've probably spelt their names wrong. Also, all the 7th formers from last year will be gone, including Clara's boyfriend, Lauren (not my sister) and Molly. Everything will be so different this year.

I'm really looking forward to the Yugoslav picnic, also I'm looking forward to going back to school, and I'm being optimistic. It's going to be a great year, yet I'll still miss the holidays. Sometimes I have mixed feelings about going back to school.

WEDNESDAY
25
JANUARY

Well, it was a great day. We went to Manukau and got some stuff and looked around. I bought two really beautiful postcards. I love postcards, I'm always buying them. We spent ages there. I searched for that Depeche Mode record I want, but couldn't find it. They had a couple of other good records there, which I should have bought.

We went to Panmure after that and I got two real nice skirts from the clothes shop next to Shanton.

Clara, Nina, and I went to the pools after that, and Mum went home. There was this real gorgeous guy there. We kept looking at each other. When he was close by, he was talking to his brothers about me and I heard one of them say, "Ask her out." I wish he did. He's real gorgeous. Pity they had to leave early.

I rang Amy up about karate. She will be starting next Thursday. I also asked her to the Yugoslav picnic and she said she'd love to go. She's got to ask her parents though.

Sometimes I feel like I can't wait for school, but I also don't want the holidays to finish. The end of the holidays are a pretty confusing time. I hope some new people will be starting the 7th form, especially boys. Amy said there will be about 340 7th formers this year. I got a shock when she said that, because there are normally only 120 that stay. She said she got a shock too when she heard it. Though, a lot will be coming back just for the camp.

I really want a boyfriend. I just need to have company, with a boy. It would be neat to go places with them. Have them over for dinner, do homework together, go to parties together or even just to walk along the beach or talk together, etc. Sorry, I got distracted by boys again.

Anyway, karate is tomorrow. I've got heaps of bruises. I've got one real huge one on my hip and another on the other side. I've got a couple on my legs and some on my arms. I just wish they would go away and that I wouldn't get them. Also, in between my fingers are bruised. That was because I punched at the same time when someone else did and our fists collided.

I want to start badminton again. I wish that it would begin soon.

My younger sister, her friend, and I are going for a ride tomorrow to get videos out. I want to see 'The Karate Warrior'. It's similar to 'The Karate Kid'.

My hair is really long now. I'm going to grow it to my waist, if I can. Well, I'm trying. I'm also trying to grow my nails. I'm doing well.

My letter to one of my pen pals was sent today. I also wrote another one to a new person in Hamilton, called Nancy. I hope everything goes well. I want to have heaps of pen pals.

I really do need a boyfriend. I wish it would be like the first term in the 4th form again. Except, this time I'll be going out with a boy. I want the whole year to be wonderful, since it's my senior year, and I want it to be the best and most memorable.

I'm really looking forward to the 7th form camp, because it's where you get to know everyone properly. Also, I'm looking forward to the ball, which I am definitely going to, and with a boyfriend. I want this year to be a success.

I really wish some great guys would start 7th form at our school. Like the guy at the pools. It's going to be neat at lunch times, because we will be allowed to go outside of school. I'm really looking forward to it. It's going to be the best.

Went to school with Shena today, so she could fix her subjects. We got two videos out afterwards, one called 'China Girl' and the other 'She's Having a Baby'. My younger sister came over for a little while (we were all at Shena's place), then Nina left to go to the pictures with her friend. I took the videos back when we finished with them, then went home. Got there about 2:26.

When I went to school today there were heaps of people starting. A lot of Japanese were there.

There are two teachers for history, Mr Hanley and Mrs Greyson. Shena's got Mr Hanley for her teacher. I hope I get him too, because he's a really good teacher. I can't wait to find out about History, because I want to look up the topics that we'll be studying and get videos out about them. I love reading History and I love learning about it too.

Only 3 days before school starts. The holidays sure went fast.

I don't have karate on Sunday, so I won't miss it even if I go to the Yugoslav picnic. Even if it was on, I would have missed it, because of the Yugoslav picnic, which I would never miss.

There is supposed to be a get together on Monday, at the beach, for some school friends. I hope I get a real good tan from the Yugoslav picnic.

My senior year at school will start in three days. I wonder what will happen in that year. Whether I get a boyfriend, become popular, or just stay the same? I don't know what will happen. And if I do get a boyfriend, what will he look like, who will he be, did I know him for a long time or is he someone I will just meet, is he nice? And so on.

I can't wait, and that's the truth. This is because I am so uncertain. I'm caught in the middle and that's why I want school to come quickly so I won't feel this way anymore, and I won't feel like I don't know what I want. When school comes I will know what I want. I'll probably fall for some guy again, but this time I want it to be different. I want guys to fall for me and me to actually have a date. I want to fill up my calendar with dates and things to do. I want guys to ring me up and ask me out. I want to be popular. Doesn't everyone? I don't want to be a nobody like in that Emily Dickinson poem 'I'm nobody! Who are you?' I saw it in the book called 'Suzy Who?' by Winifred Madison. I think I remember that poem because sometimes I feel like a nobody. And I disagree with Emily Dickinson when she wrote that it would be dull to be somebody. No, she used the word dreary. Anyway, I'd still rather be a somebody than a nobody.

The Yugoslav picnic was brilliant. The sky was cloudless and it was a beautiful day. Amy went with us. She fancied one of my cousins, but since she has a new boyfriend she didn't do anything about it.

Today, I went to the beach with Amy and some others were there. Amy's boyfriend and his friends came too, and, boy, was Amy's boyfriend Tate gorgeous. She finally hit the jackpot. He goes to a boys' school. I'm invited to a gathering of friends soon. There will be mainly Tate's friends from his school. I can't wait.

School tomorrow, nothing much to say about that. I'm more interested in meeting Tate's friends. I really want a boyfriend, and I can't wait any longer. And, I really want to get in with Tate's crowd, because they know everyone, and the boys are gorgeous.

WEDNESDAY
1
FEBRUARY

Yesterday at school, from 10:30 to 12:00, we chose our own form classes. That was great, because we stayed with our friends. And, I can't believe Mike Nicholls came back. All his friends did too, except the 7th formers from last year, although Harry Patai returned for another year as a 7th former.

I got a letter from my pen pal, the one from Hastings. She also has another pen pal who lives in my town, called Pete Samuels.

Today, I found out my classes. First I had to go to assembly, then get my stationery. After Interval I went to English. My English teacher was Mrs Haims. She's really nice. I've got to make a three minute speech about myself and present it to the class. I also had to go to the swimming pool with Clara and Jill because I'm now a liaison officer.

I had Art History after lunch. Ms Jerald was my teacher. It looks really interesting. Jake Harrison is in my class. I went to his birthday party once, that's why I know him. He's in Clara's bible class.

I had to go to my liaison class with Clara, Jill, and Tina, to introduce ourselves to the 3rd formers. After that I went home.

I went to Amy's house after school yesterday with Clara, Amy, and Jill for a talk. I stayed there for 2 and a half hours.

I also went to karate. The first half was so boring. The second half was better.

Amy is going to set me up with her boyfriend's friend, Joey Novak. One day a whole group of friends are going to get together, and we will meet. Tate, Amy's boyfriend, knows Max Sutherland.

For History, I got Mrs Greyson, which is a bummer, because Mr Hanley's class gets to go to the Bay of Islands because they're doing New Zealand History. We're doing American History. At least Amy's in my class.

FRIDAY
3
FEBRUARY

Disregard anything I said about History on Wednesday. It's brilliant, and I'm really glad I got Mrs Greyson. She's a great teacher. We're doing English History right now, around the Tudor, Stuart time. It's so interesting. I wouldn't swap the class now, even if I had the choice.

I have swapped English classes though. They had put me in the wrong one, so now instead of having Mrs Haims I've got Ms Hearse. We got a new book called 'The Grapes of Wrath'. Sounds good. There's a movie about it with Henry Fonda in it, so if I find it I'll get it out from the video shop. P.S. There was this guy in the English class with amazing blue eyes. I haven't seen him before. But I will be meeting Joey soon, so I shouldn't get distracted by another boy. But he really does have amazing eyes.

I've got my 2nd art period swapped now, since English changed around. So now I've got the two arts next to each other, then Art History, so there are three in a row.

Tomorrow we go to the Yugoslav Club because the group from Korčula is coming over to play there.

I am really, really looking forward to Monday, because that's the day I meet Joey Novak. I'm so excited and curious. You see, Amy and her boyfriend are trying to set us up, so on

Monday me and Amy are going to Tate's place to watch some videos and maybe swim, also Tate has invited some of his friends, including Joey Novak, who also likes Yugoslav girls. They have been telling him about me, and Amy has been telling me about him. I just can't wait. Joey's supposed to be gorgeous. I wonder what he would see in me, or think of me? Also, if we don't hit it off, Amy said there will be other guys there. But, I really want Joey to like me and me to like him, but him more so than me, because I really want to go out with him. He sounds perfect, plus Mum and Dad will be delighted, because he's Yugoslav. I wish Monday would come quick, I wish it was sooner.

I'm going to be graded for karate on the first Sunday of February. I'm really surprised that they are grading me so quick. I will be going to 6th kyu, which is a yellow stripe, then after that grade is the yellow belt, which I want, since I don't want to be a white belt, because when you're asked what belt you have people think you are low, just because you are a white belt, but they don't understand that there are different stages between white and yellow, instead they think it's one grade, when it isn't. So, I really want a coloured belt.

I got a letter today from a new pen pal. She's from Wellington and is the first one of the new lot that I sent off for. I sent her the Christmas card. The reason she didn't write back sooner was because she only just got back to school and got the letter a few days ago, because she's a boarder. Her name is Jennifer Auguste. There were real beautiful stamps on the letter, of birds. I've still got to send off my letter to my other pen pal, with the photo. I haven't yet got a recent picture of me, so I've got to get one quick.

There are people at my place now. They are really friendly. The Phillips and another family. We had our tea just after 8:00 because everyone was talking. It's 9:44 now and I only just had my pudding.

'Super Stars of Wrestling' is on tonight. I reckon it's funny. The wrestlers are such show offs.

I've got to exercise heaps. I will do lots tomorrow. I got my grading, school sports, and so on all coming up, so I need to be extra fit. Also, I was thinking of the triathletes tag team. I might do the running part, which is a ten mile or km run. Also, I want to look slim and good (for Joey).

SATURDAY
4
FEBRUARY

I just rang up Amy about Monday. She said that Tate is going to ask Joey about Monday at work, so I'm keeping my fingers crossed. They work at the supermarket.

Mike Nicholls walked past not long ago with his friend. Mike is still so gorgeous, but luckily I'm not hard up on him anymore, but I still like him. Luckily, I don't have a crush on anyone anymore. So, the next time I fall for someone it will be my boyfriend, and hopefully I will meet him this Monday. I can't wait.

My Guns 'n' Roses tape got all wrecked. I'm hoping that Mum can fix it when she gets home.

I don't have karate tomorrow because it's a long weekend.

The Yugoslav club tonight.

THURDAY
9
FEBRUARY

I got my first letter from a boy pen pal today. He's from the Bay of Plenty. His name is Jeremy Taylor, and he's nineteen. I was really happy to get it. He got my name from Teletex. There's a whole heap of people my age on it now.

I really love history. It is great. One of my favourite subjects. Actually, you could say it is my favourite. That shows you how much I love history. Heaps!!

Went to karate tonight. All the brown belts were back. Mike was one of them. Amy will join when some other beginners come.

I came home early from school today, because I had Study last. I also have it last tomorrow too.

I went to the 3rd formers' and liaison barbecue last night from 6-8 pm. It was good. Went for a swim, too.

Last Saturday I went with Amy to her boyfriend's house for a small party. We got there around 9:25. The people who were there was Amy, Tate, Nicky, Pete, Tate's brother, 3 other guys and Zane and me. Tate's parents stayed in the house. We were in the garage.

Talked to Zane most of the night. He likes all the stuff I like. There was also this other guy there from my school. He kept butting in and flirting with me lots. I think Zane was getting annoyed with him. I wasn't interested in the guy, but I didn't want to be rude to him, because he seemed nice enough. Still, I only wanted to talk to Zane.

Anyway, I finally went to see Joey yesterday, which I wasn't happy about. I went to the shops with Amy for the meet up, but I recognised him from a distance, so I told Amy no, I wasn't going through with it. I actually took off, because I was so embarrassed. He was from the Yugoslav club. I just didn't know his name. I felt like ringing Tate's neck, because he and Amy were trying to matchmake. I didn't blame Amy because she hadn't seen him before. Okay, I knew they were matchmaking, but they got things wrong. I won't let anyone do that again. It was so embarrassing to be set up with someone I already know! I am definitely not interested.

I hope I didn't ruin my chance with Zane, because he liked me, but couldn't ask me out on Saturday because he knew that I was supposed to meet Joey. I know he liked me, because he kept on suggesting going to the beach or concerts together. So, I'm going to ask him to come on Wednesday to badminton, because he likes the game and is supposed to be good at it. He said he played at my club before. He also does Kung Fu, so he would be interested in my karate.

I got Amy to ring Tate to get his number, also she is going to ask Tate to ask Zane whether he wants to go swimming tomorrow with us. I hope Zane says yes, but he might be doing something, because his parents just moved to Auckland on Friday. He came early because of school. He was boarding with Tate, so he might want to spend time with his parents since he hasn't seen them for so long.

What am I to do now? I'm absolutely crazy about Zane. He is just so gorgeous, but I don't know whether he's interested in me or not. I'm just praying that he is, because I am afraid that he might not like me. I acted like a jerk today. I hope he didn't go off me because of that. He is just so-o-o-o gorgeous. I really want to go out with him. I'm not thinking of any other boys now, just him. Tomorrow I'll prove it. I want him to go to badminton with me on Wednesday. Amy and Tate will be going, but it will be me who will have to phone him up and ask him out, and I'm afraid of him not liking me. I really want to be his girlfriend. I haven't got this worked up about someone for ages.

Tomorrow I'm going to make it clear to Amy that I am really crazy about him, if she doesn't already know about it. I'm going to get his number off her, which she will get from Tate. I'll be so nervous on the phone. Also Clara knows what happened today. Amy told her. I'm going to get really hassled, but I don't care as long as I get Zane. He tried to chuck me in the pool for wetting him, but I had a tank top on that I didn't want wet, so I pleaded with him not to throw me in. He didn't, but, man, I loved his arms around me. He lifted me right off the ground. He is so strong. And, boy, has he got a gorgeous bod.

Amy and Tate were all over each other and I felt embarrassed, especially when they kissed goodbye, and I mean they kissed – a long one, because Zane was right there. Man, do I wish I was kissing him. I just don't believe how much I'm attracted to him, because it came so sudden. I just can't wait to see him again. I really want him to like me, because I've got the most major crush on him. I won't even bother thinking about other guys now, and I'm going to make it clear to Amy that this is the truth and that I'm actually stuck on him, so she will know how serious I am about him, and will make it clear to Tate, so Tate will find out whether Zane likes me or not. And I pray it is the first. Please, Zane, like me and I want to be your girlfriend. I want him to hold me again. I want him to hold me as his girlfriend.

I'm going to be so nervous asking him out. Please, Zane, say yes. I reckon you're the most gorgeous, sweetest and best guy in the world. You are so spunky Zane!

I better go to bed now or else I'll be writing about him all night, and how gorgeous he is.

I wish that Mum and Nina would go downstairs so I can phone Zane. I'm nervous enough as it is.

Poor Amy. I must have bored her out of her wits today, talking non-stop about Zane. But I can't help it. I'm going to ask him whether he wants to go to badminton, and I pray that he will say yes.

I get so-o-o-o nervous when I'm going to phone a boy. I get all nervous, and get butterflies. My stomach's all tied up now. Please say yes, Zane.

Well, here goes – I'm going to phone him now.

———————————————

I rang Zane up and he said he doesn't really want to go to badminton. I felt so nervous and embarrassed, my heart was thumping full speed. I rang Amy up. I was really upset. Amy was shocked that he didn't want to go. Tate was with her. I felt so upset. At one stage I could hardly talk and get my voice straight. I'm just <u>sick</u> and <u>tired</u> of waiting to be asked out. I am never going to ring a boy again. They piss me off. I always get upset when I ring them up. It's just not fair.

Why can't boys like me for once? I just don't know what happened. He seemed to be interested in me on Saturday, but he seemed so much quieter and different on Sunday. I don't know what I did wrong. Why is it I'm the one who always seems to get hurt? Why can't everything go right for me for a change? When they say you have a crush on someone it really means exactly that: They crush you. You always seem to get hurt when you get a crush on someone. No boy ever seems to want to go out with me. Why?! What have I done? Do I have a disease or something? Because that's the way they treat me. Why do I have to be hurt so much by them? I really thought I was going to have a boyfriend this time, but as always what I really want gets taken away from me. I'm just so upset! It's not fair! Why does Amy get the pick of the bunch? She always seems to get boyfriends so easily and just look at me. What have I done wrong?! Is it because I'm too shy or just bloody ugly or a damn nuisance? I'm just so pissed off. It's not fair. Boys are such a pain. What did I ever do to them? I've never hurt them, so why do they hurt me so much?

I'm going to tell Amy just how I feel. I'm going to let her know they always seem to hurt me and why I'm so damn unlucky with them. What did I do? If I knew I could change it, but I guess I will never know. Do they want me to be more like Amy or someone else? What do I have to do to make them like me?

I could keep on forever writing like this, but it won't make a boy want to go out with me or care about me, or hold me. So, why should I bother! They're hurtful creeps.

Zane is a real good guy. Don't believe anything I said before. I was just upset. He rang me up and said that Amy and Tate rang him and said that I was upset. He said that he wasn't ready for a relationship and that he just wanted to be friends. He also kept saying sorry. He didn't want to upset me. I said it was alright. He has got such a gorgeous voice. He is such a sweet guy.

Amy also rang me up too to tell me that they rang him and wanted to know what Zane said. I told her. I only hope that Tate and Zane don't think I'm a jerk for acting like that – ringing Amy to tell her how upset I was. I just want to be around Zane whether I'm his friend or girlfriend. He is just so nice. I can't help saying all this. That is one thing about diaries; it calms you down when you're upset and makes you feel better. Also, I love to write.

I've got to go to school tomorrow, and be there at 9:00, because I have art. I have to draw some limbs models, and so do all the other 7th form art students along with the 6th formers. The rest of the school won't be coming because the teachers are having some meetings or something like that.

143

Amy and Tate are going with me to badminton on Wednesday, so that will be neat. Tate is such a nice guy to ring Zane up for me. Amy is lucky to have him.

I do want my boyfriend to be a friend. That is very important. But, I shouldn't worry about having a boyfriend anymore, I should just wait for one to ask me out and while I'm waiting I'm going to have fun and make friends, because friends are very special people.

Goodnight.

THURSDAY
23
FEBRUARY

I went to a restaurant for my brother's 21st birthday with the whole family. It was near the hospital. I liked it.

Badminton was boring yesterday, so I went home early with Nina. I think I won't do badminton this year, and instead of it I was thinking of joining Tate's modern dance class. It sounds good. He does it on Mondays. And I will at least know one person so I won't be on my own. I like dancing so I think it's a good idea to join, but first I must check it out, because I may not like it. I'll ask Amy about what she knows about the class and get her to get Tate to tell me more about it, then I can go next Monday and watch him do it.

Amy is getting bored of Tate, and she feels like dropping him. I reckon she would be crazy to drop him, he is just so nice, I wouldn't drop him, and also if I go to dancing with him I can be his friend, so I will know all his friends and be great friends with him, because he is so neat. I don't know what Amy's thinking of dropping him for; she's crazy to do that. She keeps on asking whether I would go out with him when they break up, and if he asks me, but how can I say that to her? She says she wouldn't care if I did, but I reckon she would. Anyway, Tate wouldn't want to go out with me. I reckon Tate is a very special person. I saw him today running to Amy's house when I went past in the car with my family on the way to the restaurant. He is so gorgeous; I don't know what Amy is thinking of. She wants a guy more exciting, like Max Sutherland. I'd rather have Tate. Well, I don't know Max very well, but I do know Tate, and Tate is so nice. I don't know what got into me saying those things about Zane being better than Tate the other day. That's crap. Tate is such a great guy; he was so nice to ring Zane for me. What he did made me feel better, and the poor guy, Tate, did all this when he was in big trouble with his parents, and he didn't do anything wrong. They reckon he was seeing too much of Amy, and they probably only see each other about twice or once a week. That's not much is it?

I'm going to ask Amy to ask Tate about the dancing tomorrow so I can watch the lesson this Monday. It'll be so neat. And it will be excellent because I will be seeing Tate at least once a week, so we can be great friends. I've always wanted to be friends with boys, and then if it's right he can be my boyfriend, as in a boy/girl relationship. It would be so good and it would mean that I would finally have a boyfriend. Plus, we can help each other and practise together since we will both be doing a martial art as well as dancing, and I could go over to his house a lot, and he can come over to mine. He has such a neat pool, so we can go swimming together. But, I would never steal someone's boyfriend, especially Amy's. She has got to approve of us, because I would never hurt a friend's feelings like that. It would be so unfair and mean, and I don't want to lose Amy's friendship, because she is so neat and fun, and friendly. She is a really nice person. Still, I will definitely watch Tate's modern dance lesson this Monday.

Goodnight.

FRIDAY
24
FEBRUARY

I found out Tate's not doing the dance class anymore and that it costs $100 a year, so I don't think I'll do it now, but it was still a cool idea.

On Monday the 13th we have our school camp. That's in 2 weeks' time. I thought it was in a week's time. Well, too bad. I've got to fill up my time, so it will come sooner.

Already four weeks of school has gone past now. Right now I would love to be at a party and meeting people. I'm not going to any parties or places this weekend, because Amy is visiting her uncle in the South Island.

I wish I would get some letters tomorrow; I should, because I've got about five pen pals.

At karate on Sunday the green and orange belts are going for their gradings. I should be getting my marks and certificate back from my grading soon, I hope.

I had to run off just then, because the new finch got out of the birdcage, he is in the sitting-room now. He's so hard to catch. We – Mum and I – have shut the sitting-room up so he won't get away. We'll get him later.

I went to the play 'Holy Days' on Wednesday. We saw it at the university theatre. It was the first day back for uni

148

students. Man, university is so different from college. It's just so much like an American school.

Went to pick my younger sister up with Mum at Rainbow's End where the all-night party was. It sounded really excellent, it made me want to be in it.

There is something bugging me right now, and it's not my stomach ache. It's loneliness. I need a boyfriend real bad. I'm feeling down without one and I seem to have an empty space in me that needs someone to fill it.

I think I will go and look at the modern dance class. Yes, I think I will, because I might be interested in it whether Tate is going or not. I feel like dancing. Badminton is getting boring. The kids that are going now are too young. Practically all the ones my age have left.

I want to go to Campus Life, but it's on the same time as karate on Thursday, so I'm going to have to miss a few karate lessons so I can at least go to one or two Campus Life get-togethers, and have some fun.

Boy, have I got a stomach ache. It must have been from the ride home. I think it could also have been that apple I ate.

I don't know how to get any boys at school interested in me. I've got to go places out of school to get a boyfriend.

I need a boyfriend. I do. Goodnight.

SATURDAY
25
FEBRUARY

I went to church for confession with Mum and Nina. I hate going to confession, because it makes me feel uncomfortable telling the priest what I did wrong, especially since no one wants to say those things since it's personal. And a lot of the time it's just boring stuff, like fighting with my sister. Though, it does sort of make me feel better afterwards, I just wish I didn't have to do the before bit.

Anyway, afterwards I asked around for jobs, then later on I walked to the shopping centre and got a Mother's Day card and a postcard of Piha. On the way back, I picked up my bike from Shena's, and talked to her for a little while. She passed her driver's test. She's going to give me the answers from the oral test, so that will be good.

On Monday I won't be doing any school work, only athletics. Also, I'm going to see what the modern dancing is like.

I've got church at 6:30 tonight, then at 7:30 there is the Miss New Zealand Competition. I want to watch that because a girl, who was in my class at school, is in it. I hope she does well.

For History I got a new essay to do. My last one only got 10/20 so I want to do better on this one. It's due in on the

2nd of March. I have to do it on: "The King ruled but the aristocracy governed'. To what extent is this true of the Elizabethan Period?' But instead of 'King' it really means Queen Elizabeth. I've got to look up information on the government and parliament.

I've also got my Art History task to do by Tuesday, and I must do some English by Thursday. Also, there is Art to be done by Thursday. So, there's heaps to do.

'The Henderson Kids' are on now. Kylie Minogue is in it.

WEDNESDAY
1
MARCH

I had Sports Day today. Got sunburnt and really stuffed. My legs are so stiff. I hung around with a girl called Susan. She is really nice. I won my form relay race. We had four people in it for the 4 by 100 metre run. Clara, Jemma, Carol, and I were in it. I ran last, so we finished way ahead of everyone else.

I got two letters today from my pen pals, and one yesterday too. I have to send Jeremy's card off quick, so it'll get to him in time for his birthday on Saturday.

I'm looking forward to the party on Friday night. Amy knows the guy who's having the party. It's a double birthday party. It's way out in Mt. Roskill though, which is about 30 minutes drive away. It starts at 6:00 and we will get home around 11:20 or 11:30. Something like that.

I won't hand my History essay in tomorrow, because I will be missing that period since I have to go to the Eastern Zone Athletics meeting in the hall at 3rd period. I also won't be having History on Friday, too, because we have the Liberal Studies film.

Goodnight.

MONDAY
20
MARCH

The 7th form camp was excellent. I had so much fun. Pity it was so short though. It went from Monday to Wednesday. It should have been a whole week. I took heaps of neat photos. I did abseiling – it was superb, also I did sailing, snorkelling, canoeing, etc.

Amy dropped Tate last night, and he had it coming. He was supposed to come over yesterday for a small get together with Amy, her brother, my younger sister, and I. He was also supposed to bring some friends too, then an hour after it starts he phones up to say he can't come because of homework, and we know he'd just been to Zane's. The nerve of it. That's the second time he's done it when I was around and I know he's done it heaps of other times, because Amy told me. He deserved to get dropped, the prat.

Anyway, I got tomorrow off because it's Teachers' Strike day.

I did the 40 hour famine on the weekend, which went alright.

I'm going to do my yellow belt grading in two months. It's supposed to be an honour, because I've been going regularly and have been doing well, so they are going to grade me sooner. I'm going to grade with the other girl, so I won't be doing it by myself, again.

THURSDAY
13
APRIL

I'm in a real fidgety mood. All I can think about is asking Darius whether he would like to go with us (Amy, Penelope, Cathy) to town. He's in my English class and he's also going to karate now. I first noticed him when I got moved to my new English class, because he has beautiful blue eyes. He's got cute buns too (he he). I've been a bit rude and have been making comments to my friends about his butt. I've been seeing him around a lot. He's in Mike Nicholl's group.

Penelope is bringing her boyfriend and a guy for Cathy. Amy's not sure whether she can make it because she has band practice with Mike. She is a backup singer. But all I can think of is Darius's cute smile. He didn't go to karate tonight, but I wasn't sure whether he was allowed to go. I'm going crazy. I just can't stop thinking about him. I see him everywhere. I've never felt this way before. Is he going to be another Gabriel Norton? He is just so-o-o nice. He talks to me, says "Hi" and smiles. He even gave me and Amy a lift home from karate. I've just got to go out with him. Please! Don't let this be another disappointment. Please! Let him say "Yes"! I don't think I could stand another rejection. I just can't wait till tomorrow to see him. I pray that he <u>will</u> be at school. Please, I'm getting really weird over this. I'm getting too excited.

Hyperactive. I just can't think straight. I'm always picturing Darius looking at me and smiling. Please! Let him like me. All I can think of is the first term in 4th form when Gabriel was after me, and I was too stupid to realise it until it was too late. I just hope it's a repeat excerpt this time, but with Darius as my Romeo, and him saying 'YES'!

I'm just so nervous, it's not funny. I got in this state before when I can't wait to get something done. He is going to be my first boyfriend. It's funny, I can just feel it. He just feels like he is the right one. Oh, man, it feels so much like I'm back in the 4th form. It's a rerun. Yet, I'm really scared that Darius will say no. I'm so scared I will be rejected. I <u>do not</u> want a rerun of what happened with Mike Nicholls. No, please not that again. I need to be accepted for once, <u>not</u> rejected. Please, Darius, I'm going crazy over you. Why do I always have to ask the boy out? Why wasn't Darius at karate tonight? Please say yes to me, Darius, please be my first. Darius just seems the right one. He's so special. It just seems right. It feels like he is the right one.

<u>PLEASE SAY YES!</u>

I'm still very fidgety. I've just had assembly and I'm at History now. I haven't asked him yet and I'm getting nervous. I'm scared he will say no or have work. I really want him to say yes. I just hope it's not too late to ask him. I got chicken before. I could have gone up to him and asked him, but I wanted back-up from my friends. I'll ask him, I just can't go up to him by myself. I'm getting butterflies. I want to get this over and done with. I don't know whether I can receive another blow if he rejects me. I've had it too much and I need a yes for once. I don't know whether I can take two guys in one group rejecting me. Mike rejected me. Well, it felt that way, although I didn't actually ask him out. Still, I just can't be humiliated anymore. I am so scared of being rejected. I just don't know Darius's answer and I'm very critical of myself so I'm afraid he'll say 'no'. Please let him want to go out with me.

FRIDAY
21
APRIL

He said YES! This was a week ago now, and I'm going out with him. He is so gorgeous. He is my first boyfriend. I'll tell you what happened from last Saturday onwards.

Well, on Friday when I asked him out, I was shaking like crazy. I hope he didn't notice, but it didn't matter, because he said YES! I asked him in the school library. I almost chickened out, because I've never asked a guy to his face before, only over the phone. But a girl I know, who's going out with his best friend, stopped me from backing out. She encouraged me, and I'm so grateful, because I expected, like with Zane, for him to say no. BUT he didn't!

So, on Saturday I got all done up to look good for Darius. He was bringing a friend along too. He asked me the night before on the phone (Friday the 14th). Anyway, he was supposed to come to my house at 1:00, but he didn't realise that it was so far to walk here, so at 1:20 Cathy rang me up to say that our lift had gone, her dad, because he had to go to work, and since I couldn't wait any longer, my Mum and I went looking for Darius and his friend. We found them walking up the road. We picked them up, then went straight to Cathy's place, but it was the wrong house. Amy told me it was 202, but it was really 212. She had mistakenly got the wrong

158

number from Cathy. Because of this, I had to walk around for ages, trying to find Cathy's house and in the end I went to the real estate agents across the highway so I could ring home to get her number, so I could find her house. When I finally got her address I went back to the car where Mum, Darius, and Anthony were, and I kept on saying sorry all the time. I was so embarrassed. Darius was a good sport about it.

After all of this, we finally went and picked up Cathy, then Mum drove us all to Darius's house so we could get his car, because we had no other way to get into town. When we got to his place, he got his keys and we all piled into his car. I saw his twin brother. They look heaps alike, except for their hair. Next, Darius then drove us in, but we couldn't find the others, and since we were ¾'s of an hour late, we went to the pictures straight away. We got there just as it started; it was 'Naked Gun'. The film was stupid, but it was worth being there with Darius. Afterwards, we went to McDonalds, then to a record shop, then we walked around looking at other shops. When it was time to go, we all piled into Darius's car and drove home. We dropped Cathy off first, then Darius asked me to a party. He'd asked me earlier, but he told me all about it properly. I said that I wasn't sure, because Mum and Dad were going out and I had to look after my younger sister, but I would ask and see. So, he dropped me off at the fish and chip shop so I could get Nina's and my tea. Then we said goodbye.

After I got the chips, I walked home and partly ran. As I was going up the hill, I was thinking of how I could persuade Mum to let me go to the party, but when I got home I found Dad was the only one there. He told me that Nina may have broken her shoulder by falling off her skateboard, and that Mum had taken her to the hospital. When they came back, we found out that it was a broken arm at the top. So, that crossed out all my chances of going to the party. I was really afraid that Darius wouldn't want to go out with me again because of all the cufufal (I have no idea how to spell that word) with what happened before being in town. But that was not so, because the next day after karate he came up to me and asked me why I wasn't at the party. I explained about what had happened with my sister and he offered me a lift. I had my bike, but he said it was alright and put it in the boot of his car. He then drove me home, and when we got there he helped me get my bike out, and then asked me out for next week. I was thrilled. I said yes of course. As soon as he left, I went around the corner and jumped for joy. My first boyfriend!

The next day at school I had English first and I met him there. After English he waited for me, and we walked over to the assembly for the Board of Education candidates of students. He sat with me. Once assembly was finished, we walked to our classes and said goodbye. I had History. At Interval everyone was asking about my date with Darius. They were thrilled. At third period we went to assembly again and listened to more candidates. Me, Amy, and the others were sitting across the hall from Darius, because he came in late, and Amy said he kept looking at me. She reckons he likes me heaps. I hope so. Everyone at school knows we're going out together now, and if they don't they will soon.

Well, on Wednesday he gave me a lift to the pictures for Liberal Studies. We had English before lunch, and I went to sit with him and his group for a little while. Darius, me, and his friend Anthony went to the pictures. We picked up two other guys on the way and gave them a lift. Darius had seen the film 'The Mission', which we were seeing, so he went home. But, before he left I gave him my number.

'The Mission' was good. It was sad, but it had beautiful photography. I walked home after it.

Darius was at karate on Thursday and we talked. He didn't go to karate on Tuesday, because he had to study for a test.

Today we talked heaps and laughed. He was so-o-o gorgeous today. I couldn't keep my eyes off him. Before he went to roll call, me and Amy ran over to ask him whether he wants to go to Rainbow's End on Tuesday. Amy will be going with Mike (not Nicholls) and I will be with Darius. We will get a lift with Amy's mum. He said YES! So that will be excellent. I will tell him all the details on Sunday at karate. I hope he phones me or asks me out for any day.

I like him HEAPS and I reckon he is GORGEOUS!

Shena has left school. She got a job in a bank. Her final day was last Wednesday. She starts work on Monday the 24th, which means she won't be walking to school with me anymore, because she will be working. But, I will still see her. One day we will watch her 'Superstars of Wrestling' tape. I can't see it this weekend because I'm so busy.

TUESDAY
2
MAY

I want to see Darius right now. I really like him heaps, and heaps, and heaps, etc. On Saturday, me and Darius went to see 'Dangerous Liaisons', a really good movie about mistresses and lovers, and deceit. It was complicated, and had a sad ending. Amy was there too, but by herself, because the other guys - Cathy, Penelope, Tarj, and Simon didn't show up. So, after the pictures Darius, me, and Amy piled into Darius's car and he dropped her off first then me next. He asked whether I would like to come over to his house for a video at 7:00, and of course I said "Yes". I went and met his mother, stepfather, and his two cousins: one of them is Seth, who was in my younger sister's class last year. We watched the film 'Overboard' with Goldie Hawn in it.

I went for my yellow belt grading on Sunday with Lana. We both passed and now I'm a coloured belt! The black belt who took us said that it was the best grading he has seen for our grade. I got bruises all the way up my left arm and on my knuckles from the ten fights we had to do.

I'm going to the neighbouring college tonight at 7:30 for the careers evening. Tomorrow I don't have English, so I'm going to talk to Darius at lunchtime. I should have done that today. I really like him.

I got the job at the department store Kendals. I'll be working on Fridays from 5:00 to 9:00 and Saturdays from 9:30 to 12:00 or 12:30. So, at least I'll have some cash. I probably will be working in the holidays too, but not all of the holidays – or they wouldn't be holidays!

(Written on a piece of paper, and left in my diary)

I should stop worrying about Darius not wanting to go out with me anymore. I'm getting paranoid, which is mainly because Mum won't let me go to that party he invited me to. The problem is that it's an overnight one just outside of Auckland. But I still really, really want to go, so I'm going to ask her again. Tomorrow I have English first, so I'll talk to Darius about it and see what's happening. Also, I hope he wants to do something in the holidays. My mind's all in a muddle. I just need to be with him, so I know that he likes me and I don't have to worry. I wish my paranoia would go away, so I can relax for once.

I'm tired right now. I'm in Art History and my head's all funny. I'm just so tired. I wish I could get into Art History, but I find it immensely boring. I need something to occupy me. I hope I get some letters from my pen pals today. I should get into my work so I won't keep thinking of other things, especially that damn party I'm not allowed to go to.

I've got my job this Friday, so I can't do anything with Darius that night. It's my first day on the job. At least now I will have some cash coming in.

The Ball's coming up soon and I'm praying that Darius will ask me. I want him to get serious about me, have a relationship, not just go places together sometimes and when we pass say "Hi". I want us to be together a lot. But I guess that takes time. I should be pleased that he actually wants to go out with me. And everyone says he likes me. It's just my paranoia that is getting to me.

I better do some Art History now.

Written in my diary...

Forget what I said on that piece of paper, I was just paranoid. It's true, but I feel better now, because I went to the library the last fifteen minutes of Art History and Darius was there. I worked there till the bell went, then put stuff away and went to get my backpack. Well, Darius came up to me and we walked together to my art room. He asked what I was doing at the weekend and Friday. I told him I was working on Friday, so he said he'd think of something to do. We can't do anything on Saturday night because he's going to THAT party, the one I'm not allowed to go to. What a bummer. Anyway, I'll talk to him about it at English, which is first. Still, I was so happy when he was talking to me and I'm so happy now, too, because he wants to see me and go out together this weekend. We could also go somewhere in the holidays. Just the two of us. He is

166

just so-o-o nice, and he's gorgeous. He's the nicest boy I know. Well, he isn't exactly a boy, he's nearly nineteen.

I, for my ambition, would like to become a black belt and take my own classes. I know it will take years, but I have the determination to do it. I really like karate. Right now it's the only thing I do know I like, besides Darius. Darius is gorgeous.

We just had a Limbs concert in the hall for the 6th and 7th formers' last period. It was good. They announced at the end of the concert that the ball will be on the 16th of June, and that tickets will be on sale as soon as everyone comes back from the May holidays. The tickets separately are $35 each and a double ticket is $68. So, it's time for everyone to ask each other to the ball. I want Darius to ask me.

I got karate tonight, so I will be getting my actual yellow belt. I will swap my old white belt for the yellow one. Darius won't be there, probably because he has a calculus test tomorrow. He has it first period.

I wonder whether I will try out for the army. It sounds interesting. It takes 6 months to get in though. Tomorrow is the last day at school before the holidays. We only have 3 periods tomorrow. Mine are Study first – I'll probably write letters in that period, then there is English with Darius, and last

History. This term has gone so fast. It's incredible. And it's the longest one, too. I wonder what will happen next term.

FRIDAY
12
MAY

I'm a confused kid. My head is in a muddle. Well, I'll tell you what happened during the time we finished school, from last Friday to now.

On Friday night I had work, which started at 5 and finished at 9. It was my first time at Kendals department store. The people who work there are very nice, heaps nicer than at the last department store I worked at when I was younger.

After work Mum, Dad, and Nina all came to meet me and take me home. Then I got changed to go to Anthony's house for the spa. Mum took me down and I met Darius, Anthony, and Lena there. At about 9:30 we went in the spa and came out at 11:30, which meant I got home late. I was supposed to be home by 11:30 pm at the latest.

On Saturday, I went to work from 9:30 to 12:30. At night I went to Shena's house at 7:00. I told Shena what had happened since she'd left school and we watched the movie 'Little Nikita', it was good, then we watched some 'Superstars of Wrestling'. Shena and her father took me home at 10:30 pm.

The next day I went to church by myself and then to karate. I was in a grouchy mood after karate and I went to sleep for a while. I rang Lena about the party that I wasn't allowed to go to. I wanted to know what had happened, and I also wanted to have all three of them over for a video, well at least Darius, but Lena said they would be sleeping because they were all tired.

I had REALLY wanted to go to that party, so all weekend and before it I couldn't get it out of my head, because I was pissed off that I wasn't allowed to go.

On Monday I went to work at the cafe, where Mum sometimes helps out, from about 11:00 to 3:30. I got $22.50 out of that.

At night I rang Darius up to see whether he wanted to have a swim at the pools and then get a video the next day. He said "Yes". We had a great time on Tuesday, me and Darius. We got 'Saigon' out. It was a good video. He left about 5:30. I think he asked me out for Wednesday to go to town. After he left I was in a really good mood and didn't feel confused at all. I went to karate and I was grinning all night.

On Wednesday the 10th I went to town with Darius. We caught the bus at about 9:30 and when we got to town we looked around the shops. He got a David Bowie tape. We went to see 'Tequila Sunrise' next. It was an excellent movie. It had Mel Gibson, Michelle Pfeiffer, and Kurt Russell in it. After the movie we went to Victoria Park Market, and on the way we passed an old girlfriend of Darius's and her sister. At Victoria Park Market we looked around, had some lunch and then went to the park across the road. After that we walked back up to the main part of town and looked through a huge shop, then walked to the wharf. Before that Darius got some ice cream for me and himself, and we tried to push the ice cream into each other's nose. At the wharf we sat down at the edge and talked like before, then he climbed this thing to see whether he could get up it. While we were there, he asked whether I wanted to go to his mother's wedding on the last Saturday before school. I said "Yes". We then walked back to catch a bus, and he started talking about the ball. But, he hasn't asked me to it yet, but it sounded like it was going that way. Maybe he will ask the next time he sees me.

We caught a bus straight away when we got to the station, and on the way home we talked a lot. I pulled the cord just before the Intermediate, where I was going to get off. Darius didn't know I was getting off there and I didn't know he wasn't getting off at the same stop, so I nearly walked off the bus without saying "bye" to him, but luckily I turned to look behind me and saw him down the end of the aisle smiling at me. I said "bye" from where I was and got off the bus. I hope he doesn't think I'm an idiot for doing that, but I didn't know he wasn't getting off there. I hope he realised what happened.

Well, I walked home and got there at 4:50. From then on I became confused, going over what I had done. But I had an excellent day out with Darius. He's excellent.

The next day I went with Mum and Nina to the hospital at 8:30, so Nina could get her arm checked. After that we went to Shanton and other places on Cavendish Drive, then to Manukau Shopping Centre. I got a really choice vinyl jacket there. It was $59. Then we had lunch and looked around some more shops. I couldn't find anything I could wear to Darius's mum's wedding. After Manukau we went to Deka and got a nice ice cream at Big Fresh. I posted my letter, then we drove to my great grandmother's house, where we stayed for a while. My grandfather and one of my cousins were also there. We then went home, returning around 4:00, maybe 3:30.

That night I went to karate, hoping to see Darius, but he wasn't there. At karate I was in a foul mood, but at the last bit I became happier and started mucking around. Dad picked me up after it was finished and we went home.

I had tea and watched T.V. After that I went to bed at 12:15, because I watched the funny British movie called 'St. Trinian's'.

So, now it's Friday, nearing the end of another week and I'm confused again. Half of our holidays are nearly over.

Darius is leaving tomorrow to go up north to see his father and will be gone for about 5 days at the most, because he has to be back in time for his mum's wedding. I hope he phones me so I can see him before he leaves. I want to at least talk to him, so I won't be confused anymore, because I can get confused by anything no matter how big or small it is.

He also has to tell me when the wedding starts, etc. He'll probably tell me that when he comes back from seeing his dad and little brother and sister. His younger brother and sister are only babies.

SATURDAY
27
MAY

I'm so nervous that I can't even write properly now. I always get nervous when I ring a boy, even if he is my boyfriend.

Well, the wedding went great. Darius rang up on Tuesday and we were on the phone for two whole hours. Actually, the wedding was brilliant, everyone in Darius's group talked to me and it was like I had been in that group for ages. I even talked to Mike Nicholls, the one I used to have a crush on, and I wasn't embarrassed. I like Darius so much. Darius's brother Sebastian gave his mother away at the wedding because her father is dead. Darius's other brother Brent is so funny.

I went to bed about 12:20.

All this week I sat with Darius's group. And on Monday, when we had Liberal Studies, we did ballroom dancing. I danced with Darius. He's a real good dancer.

Anthony had his last day of school on Friday, because he's going to do a journalism course. At the end of lunch I got him covered with heaps of stinking talcum powder, dumping it down the back of his shirt and on his hair. It was so-o-o funny. He tried to get everyone else covered in it. The others were supposed to bring eggs and shaving cream, but they forgot.

Well, I'm going to try and ring Darius up again because there was no answer before, and I want to ask him to the pictures tomorrow, because 'Young Guns' is on and I really want to see it, also I want to go somewhere with him.

Darius is going to the ball with me! Yey! Hopefully we will be going nightclubbing after it with the Afterball.

I hope he answers the phone when I ring, because I want to speak to him and know that he still likes me. Sorry about that, I get paranoid sometimes. He must like me to want to go out with me, so why do I get paranoid like this?

The 14th of April was when I first asked Darius out and he said "Yes". The 15th of April was our first date. That is nearly 6 weeks we have been going out together and we haven't even kissed. I'm going to have to start getting randy or something. He's put his arm around me and some other things, but hasn't kissed me yet. Well, he gnawed my hand a bit, but it wasn't a kiss. Anyway, wish me luck as I'm going to ring again.

———————————

No answer, no one's home. I'm going to try again later on. I wonder where he is?

So much stuff has happened since I last wrote, and I am really stupid for not having written sooner. First thing I want to write about is the <u>Ball</u>. It was on the 16th of June and it went great, although it went by too fast. The band was great, the food was great, everything was great, and Darius was gorgeous. But I felt a bit self-conscious because of my hair. It had been permed on the Monday before the Ball, then on the day it was set in rollers, which meant I had no fringe – it felt all funny, I didn't like it.

Yesterday a group of us, about 20 altogether, went to Valentines at 6:30, then into town to see the movies. We saw 'Married to the Mob'. I liked it a lot. Michelle Pfeiffer acted in it. Brilliant. We went to the Manukau bowling alley after that and stayed there till about 11:20, then my older sister took Darius and me home. This was all for Diana's birthday.

Did I tell you my older sister is engaged? Great aye! She is going to marry Phillip, my future brother-in-law, next year on the 10th of February, and I'm bridesmaid. Their engagement party is tonight, just for the relations.

I have now been going out with Darius for 3 months from yesterday. His birthday is at the end of this month. It's funny reading over what I wrote ages ago, because a lot of

177

things are different now. It's especially funny reading about Darius not having kissed me. Well, that situation has changed. Amy reckons at first kissing is horrible or gross, but after a little while it is wonderful and you can't do without it. Well, it was definitely weird at first, really awkward, but I still liked it. But I suppose she would know more about it than me. Anyway, I actually kissed Darius first. I was so nervous, but decided I wasn't going to chicken out, because I didn't want to wait any longer, so when Dad dropped him off at his house, I told Dad I wanted to walk Darius to the door, and because it was in a place Dad couldn't see, I kissed Darius there. I don't think Darius was expecting it, and I did it fast, sort of got him half on his lips and half off. I was so nervous, but I still did it! And now he kisses me all the time.

But I'm unsure about things at the moment. School's not going well, and I just want it over, I've had enough of it. I'm sick of my subjects, and I think it's affecting everything, because I've also got mixed feelings about Darius. I suppose one second you can't do without them – boys – and the next you can. Well, I hope everything turns out for the best, because he is really nice.

It's weird being popular now, and I am. I'm part of a big group. I'm invited to heaps of parties and I can't believe all this is happening to me. The group I'm in is the group I wanted to be in all of 6th form, and now I'm in it and have a boyfriend. I used to feel a fool around these people last year, and now they are my friends. It's freaky. Still, I'm not happy with school, not with my group and it probably isn't with Darius either, it really is the study that I'm not liking. I reckon I'm failing Bursary, or I should say I'm going to, and everything is so-o-o different from all the other years. I don't want to fail, and to pass my subjects I'm going to have to do a lot less social stuff, and a whole lot of work. I've changed, I really have changed.

Amy really pisses me off sometimes – it's like she ignores me. I think it's because I sit with Darius's group now, not with her, and she's jealous. Well, now I'm on a roll, I'm going to make heaps of new friends and be the most popular person in the 7th form and the college.

WEDNESDAY
26
JULY

That is all shit about wanting to be the most popular person and so on; I just get carried away sometimes when I write. And forget what I said about Amy, things change and if she wanted to sit with me she would. I guess it's like when Clara used to sit with her boyfriend, and I used to get annoyed, so I shouldn't get annoyed with Amy for feeling the same way. She has every right to. So be it. Things happen and you can't change them, just as long as we still stay friends.

Anyway, I'll get to the actual reason why I'm writing in my diary right now. I'm getting real pissed off because at school this week all I've done is be a nuisance. It's because I get so bored. I'm really afraid that Darius is losing interest in me. Well, I guess I will see tomorrow whether I'm paranoid or not. But I'm really afraid that he might be. Tomorrow I must be more mature and sexy, and not an immature nuisance. I am really getting fed up with my stupidness. It's pissing me off. Well, here's the plan for tomorrow.

THURSDAY

Art History (me) – Study (him)
Study (me) – Maths (I think he has this?)

Interval

English together

Lunch

Liberal Studies together
History (me) – Physics (him)

Well, when I get to school I'll go to the library for roll call. Actually, no, I won't, I think we have assembly first so I'll meet Darius there and be randy. If we don't have assembly then I will pass him by when he goes to study and slap his butt. Hold around waist if assembly, etc. Also, when I go to the library for study after Art History, slap as before. Interval – hands caress or hold. English – same.

When lunch comes hint at going home. More there. Liberal Studies we will probably be doing a tug-o-war, because if it rains we can't do soccer – pity. History next and ride home after. Talk about his birthday and present – don't tell him what it is though. Talk about dinner at the carvery.

Please don't let him lose interest in me. I've got to do something – not be such a stupid nuisance.

Wear same jeans and red T-shirt with green hooded top and cream jumper, and either blue jacket or denim one. Same shoes.

I'm really, really scared that he will drop me, so I must get my mind onto something else like homework, and work non-stop till I see him, and then I will make him want me so badly – he has me, but he hasn't done anything so I'm going to make him randy and eager. Well, we have been going out for 3 and almost a ½ months. That is a long time and it's going to be even longer, much longer.

Tomorrow, I'm going to make him want me so much. To do something very special for me and him. He is my first boyfriend and so I want to be both his girlfriend and his best close friend. I want to be so-o-o close to him. That settles it – no more immatureness. I will be mature and sexy for him. I can't be gutless, so I will do what I plan to do. I can't chicken out this time, I'm going to be firm and not betray my wishes because of gutlessness. I'm going to do what I say.

I promise!

THURSDAY
27
JULY

Everything's alright. Forget about my paranoia and stupidity.

FRIDAY
28
JULY

Everything's brilliant.

I PASSED BURSARY!

1. I'm still going out with Darius.

2. I've been accepted to the 18 weeks tech course.

3. I'm working full time at Kendals during the Christmas holidays.

4. I'm bloody sunburnt!

Well, at least no more worries for a while. I'll write later.

Diary 1990

MONDAY
1
JANUARY

It's 1990! Tomorrow I will be going to the beach with Mum, Nina, and Penelope.

Tomorrow night I will be with Darius. He is coming over at 8:30 after work. It's a pain that he has to work tomorrow, just when I get my holidays and can do something. He is moving out of his house this Friday to a new place. I want to help out on Saturday.

I've only got 2 more weeks of work left and I can't wait till it's finished. Darius is back to working at his old job on Wednesday.

I went to a New Year's party last night, but I couldn't do what I wanted that day, because I was really sick from four in the morning onwards because of a stomach bug. I was vomiting and had diarrhoea. Awful aye!

Mike Nicholls and Liam Hudsworth will be going back to karate on Sunday, so it will be a lot more fun now. I really like karate heaps. They are going to be there for about a year so they can get their black belt, because if they don't go back they will lose their brown belts.

I don't much like talking over the phone, because it's not really private, anyone can listen into your conversation, and you can't say all the things you want just in case you might get into trouble with your parents because they are within earshot.

Now I have to hide my diary because I'm going to get more personal. I know I'm already doing personal stuff, but this time I'm actually going to write about the people close to me and around me. And if they read it both of us could be hurt. I'm not going to say anything awful about them, because I couldn't, I love them, and wouldn't hurt them in any way. I know what my older brother and sister did was wrong in Mum's and Dad's eyes and I would never hurt my parents deliberately. I believe what Lauren did wasn't totally wrong, but also not totally right either. She may have needed to get away and be independent, but she did it with the wrong person, but everyone makes a mistake and I'm no exception, so it was her decision to make. And how would she have known that the guy she flatted with was the wrong person, and anyway she was definitely old enough to move out, it's just that my culture is strict, and you're not supposed to move in with a guy unless you have married them. My older sister is a lovely person, so she wouldn't have wanted to upset my parents, but ... I don't know, things can be hard sometimes. You want to do something, but you know it may upset other people. I suppose that's why I keep my thoughts in here and don't say them to people. It's just hard to please everyone, including yourself.

Anyway, I'm really looking forward to this year at tech, and all the other experiences that I will be having. Though, I'm still confused about my relationship with Darius, but I know I do care for him a lot. I must, because I always want to be with him. I know he likes me heaps too, because he told me more than once in different ways and he is not one for saying things he doesn't really mean. I also think he is more serious about me than any of his previous girlfriends, and that he wouldn't hurt me. He's always saying things that are flattering, and I would be lying if I didn't say that I was flattered.

I don't know whether I should write some of the things I want to in this book, because if it gets read I would be in big trouble and they are only thoughts and feelings, and I don't believe one should probe into another's feelings and thoughts, because only that person should know about them, unless they specifically want to tell anyone that is close to them, although they might want to hide it from these people specifically.

I'm a bit scared of going to tech, but excited too, because it's something new and unknown to me, and I'm unsure whether I can match up to it. I really hope I can cope with all the workload, because it's supposed to be really pressured, a million times more than the average school, especially since it's for such a short time (18 weeks), so more things will be crammed into it. There are only 18 people doing

189

the course, and I'm curious, not to say the least, and I will definitely be nervous when I go. Getting into tech and being with Darius are both boosts to my morale and confidence. Tech proved that I am a good artist, because I was only one of 18 who were accepted from 130 or so people for the course, so they must have been impressed with my work.

Everything has worked out really well, because if I didn't base my art in 1989 on a patterning style I may never have gotten into tech, since this is the type of work they associate with graphics, which means I'm suited for their course. At least I know I'm good for something. And I'm the only one in our family out of us kids to actually go for a career that was my number one choice, not second best, but my first and upmost wish. I want to be a graphic artist with my own studio and assistant. I want to do well in my career too. Also, Darius wants to do well in his career. He wants to be a lawyer and a millionaire by the end of this decade, and he is actually really serious about it. It's mainly because of the way he was brought up that makes him really want to do well in his career, because of the tough times.

Darius is also proof that I'm not unattractive to males like I tried to make out last year, and all those years before. There were others who liked me, but I was always naive, and I'm probably still naive, but in a different way. Gabriel Norton found me "Spunky" in his word, and I regret not going out with him, but I was only a 4th former with no knowledge of what boys were like, and anyway, the memory would probably be better than the real thing if he turned up now. Actually, I'm not sure I totally believe that, but I have Darius, so it doesn't matter. He's all I need.

Also, Zane confused me at the beginning of last year. He liked me at first then just led me on. But the way Amy went on about him later, I think he regretted not going out with me. He wished I was at that party and asked after me. I bet he might think of me like I think of Gabriel, but not as strongly. But Gabriel is a memory, while Darius is the present, and hopefully the future too.

I'm back to the subject of embarrassment. It's funny too, because of the song that is now playing on the radio. 'Wild Thing' by Tone Lōc. But I don't think of sex like the song does. It's precious and I believe you got to be in love when you do it and if you're in love you should be married, or intend on being with each other for the rest of your life, and that should be a marriage. I wonder why males want sex more than girls. I think Darius does. He says that if he goes too far with me that I should tell him, because he never wants to hurt me and I respect him for that. I hope he respects me (he should, especially since he treats me so nicely). I can tell he wants sex by his hints and joking suggestions and actions. Actually, now when I think of it I'm quite sure he wants it, he just said tonight that it is up to me. I won't do it fully now anyway, because of pregnancy scares before marriage and because it isn't right, not at this moment anyway. Just doesn't feel right. It would be like I'm cheating on myself. It may sound selfish, but it's the truth. I would be cheating Darius, too. When I do, do it, it is going to be right for everyone and mostly for myself and the one I love. Man, these songs on the radio love talking about sex. If these songs were played in the 1960s or 50s the artist and DJ would probably be arrested. Finally a good song. I love this song now by Belinda Carlisle. Her whole LP is brilliant.

Well, back to the subject I was talking about, or should I say 'writing'. Penelope wants to hear about it tomorrow. You could say she is my best friend, and you could say that I confide in her, and you would be right. She is more mature than me in most ways, but I still believe that I am mature in my own way too. I'm not immature because I haven't had sex, and I really believe because I haven't had it that I am more mature. It proves that I am not a flittish idiot of a girl. It also shows responsibility. I think Penelope is really nice, but she gets more carried away than me, not like Amy, though. She gets carried away in a serious way, but it's all too fast. It's probably her upbringing and earlier experiences with boys than me. My culture is different and if it wasn't I might be like her now if I had her experience. I'm not saying what she did is wrong, no way, no one but herself can say whether it is wrong or not, and no one can say what I do is wrong or not, because I believe in myself and I know I'm not an irresponsible person, and I don't do anything on the fling. My upbringing made me feel this way, and I now know whether something is acceptable or not. I know that my upbringing is strict and I respect that. It shows that my parents care enough for my well-being and that they love me. Also, they must be scared that I will do what my older brother and sister did and they will do anything to prevent it. Although I can't say what my siblings did was wrong or right, that's not my decision to make, plus everyone has different opinions. The average Kiwi probably would think what they did was fine, but my family aren't the average Kiwis. Still, I believe I won't do what my brother and sister did, because I am my own person and I do have my own feelings that are individual and uncopied, and I will do what I believe is right in my own unique individual way, and that will be without any hurt feelings within my family, because I love them too much to hurt them, and I don't think they can take another child of theirs going in a direction that they object to. I want them to be proud of me, and I want me to be proud of myself and my actions, so I must do what feels right. I love my family and parents and I will never hurt them intentionally or unintentionally.

I better stop writing now because everyone has gone to sleep, and I'll probably write some more tomorrow. I won't make any resolutions now, because:

1. I can't think of anything and

2. I know what I want to be like and things will come naturally.

I'll just say that the resolutions I made last year came true.

TUESDAY
2
JANUARY

(And, yes, I still can't believe it's 1990)

It doesn't feel like 1990, and it didn't feel like Christmas before. A lot of people said the same thing. It may be because everything changes as we get older. It doesn't feel like anything special now – it feels weird.

I just made a pudding before. I need to learn to cook more, because I'm getting to the age where I need to know how to cook.

I didn't go to the beach in the end, due to the stuffed weather. Instead, I stayed home and watched a good movie called 'Weird Science' with Nina and my two cousins, Tasha and Marija, who are staying another night.

I can't wait till my full-time work at Kendals finishes. It would be great to be free of responsibilities for a couple of weeks.

I don't feel like writing any more, maybe I'll write more tomorrow.

I feel awful. I feel like going to bed and crying and crying. Why? Because I'm a stupid fucking idiot. We were supposed to go to Long Bay today for the Foodtown Picnic and Darius, Aunty Vesna, and some others were supposed to come. But Darius phoned up and said he couldn't make it, because he had forgotten he'd already made plans with his brother to go to the speedway. All I did on the phone was say "Hm, hm, hm." I couldn't tell him that I was hurt or anything. The reason why I was going "Hm, hm, hm," all the time was because if I said anything else my voice would have cracked and I would have cried. Well, I did when I put the phone down. I was really looking forward to the picnic today. He probably didn't realise, but I was.

APRIL

(Typed on a piece of paper with no date. Due to the Easter and green belt references, I'm making an assessment that this must've been typed in April, 1990)

Diary...

Tomorrow I'm getting up at about 5:50 in the morning, because at 6:20 Darius, Brent, and Lisa are coming over to pick me up to go to the island where Darius and Brent's father lives. We are to catch the ferry at 7:45. I'm hoping that it won't rain because that will be a real bummer; also I'm hoping that Darius is feeling better and that his bug will be gone.

Yesterday I went to Deka to buy heaps of Easter eggs for both my younger sister and me, but it was mainly for Nina.

Next Sunday, I will be doing the green belt grading for karate. In this grading, I will have to break wooden boards, one with my hand and the other with my foot. Also, I will have to do 20 fights, which are about one and a half minutes each, and done one after the other. The people who I will be fighting range from white to black belts (and everything in between). I will have to fight mainly the really high grades and they will be really trying to get us bad. Also, there will be other things to do such as techniques, continuous techniques, and tarnran (don't know the correct spelling). Tarnran is something done really hard for 4 minutes, it's for spirit. I also have to do a theory paper too, but that's at home. It will take about another three years to get my black belt, because you can't get it under five years. I've been going to karate now for two years on Tuesday, Thursday, and Sunday, and have done one karate camp, which lasted the weekend and was very hard.

SATURDAY
5
MAY

I want things that I cannot have, not materialistic things, but the right to think for myself and do my own thing, not to be tied up so much that I'm too weak to say what I feel because I know it's damn useless to say anything. People want to run all over other people's lives and those other people are afraid to cause hurt to those they love, the hurt which was caused by others who came before them. Me? Number 3 in the middle. The nervy one. Number one – the oldest left home to be with another, an alien to my parents, one who did not share the family's ideals and views. She left and caused hurt, hurt that was one more burden to number 3. Always trying hard to do what both sides of her wanted caused 3's ideals and feelings and wants to clash. But before number 1's choices, even bigger problems came from number 2, the one who was meant to take over our father's role, but cannot through no fault of his own. Not because he can't, but because it goes against who he is, who he wants to be, how he wants to live. But, this clashed with our parents' hopes and dreams for him, which ended in rebellion, causing him to break free to live a life our parents can never understand.

Family drives you nuts sometimes, especially when you're feeling sick and tired. Last night I went over to Darius's house to see the film 'Aliens' and it was brilliant, a lot like 'Leviathan', which was absolutely brilliant. Well, forget about the films, OK! Darius really cares for me and I think, no, I won't say it yet, but I really like him heaps and I really mean it. He's the first person to really come close to me and want to know my feelings. He wants to know how I feel about us and what we do. He said that he doesn't deserve me, and that I'm too nice for him, but he is so nice and caring, gorgeous, intelligent, and everything else. He wants to have sex with me, but won't pressure me because he knows I'm scared of pregnancy and what it would do to my family. I can't hurt my family, especially Mum and Dad, who are so vulnerable now, especially after my brother's departure, and my older sister leaving to go live with her boyfriend. Darius would love me to live with him, but both Darius and I are thinking realistically: for one thing it would be too expensive, and another is that I can't hurt Mum and Dad by leaving, especially when I know how they felt about Lauren's departure. I know that they love me, but it does feel like I'm trapped, even more so since they are still trying to run Lauren's life and she's almost 24. I can't stay at home forever. They expect me to stay at home till I get married, but Darius doesn't want to get married to anyone. He thinks it's old tradition, so eventually he'll want to live with me and what can I do but to say no. I think I love Darius, but it's a new type of love, so I'm still unsure.

SATURDAY
9
JUNE

Mum and Dad have come back from holiday and I feel awful. I'm not going to trust Lauren again, but, bloody hell, as usual the same thing will happen over and over again. I will probably forgive her because I'm a bloody sucker. She was babysitting me and my sister, and dobbed us in when we went out, me to see Darius and Nina to see her friend. I'm 18! I should be allowed to go out with my boyfriend without having to check in.

Before all of that, this week was actually good, and I didn't want the weekend to come. I admit I was very sore on Thursday and also Friday, because of my period, but I felt a little free since my parents weren't home, not counting when Lauren was behind my back. Although, whenever Nina happens to be with Darius and me, I always get upset. I get put down so much. That's one thing Darius doesn't do, is put me down. He got upset when Nina did it to me and even more when he found out about me getting in trouble with my parents, and that really means something to me. Mum is now saying that she doesn't trust me because I went out when they were away, after having trusted me all the times before. What the heck?! I have to do so much because I'm too scared, and I mean scared to do what I want, because it means my parents

202

will get hurt. I can't win either way. Darius has asked me to live with him because he cares a heck of a lot for me. Automatically what Mum and Dad will think is that we will be up to no good. Mum said there would be no future with him if he doesn't want to marry. He is a human being I care greatly for and both of us are bordering on the line you could call love. He said he was unsure of it, so am I, but he said that his best friend asked him whether he loved me and he said to me that he liked me so much and that he could even say it was love, but to admit he is in love is such a great thing, because he actually said he didn't believe in saying it because he hadn't known it before, but when he said that to me it was like saying that I had changed his mind about it and that he would fall in love with me. I'm scared of everything. I'm a nervous person who looks out for everyone else but myself and it drives me crazy. It makes me so scared that I'm unable to do what I want because it clashes with other people's feelings and wants. My parents lived a different life when they were children and they cannot ever imagine how I feel. They can't! I feel sometimes that I've been bullied, picked on by my younger sister and older brother, then sucked up to afterwards, and with Mum and Dad's pressure of not being allowed to do what I need to do is so hard. Because I'm the 3rd child I'm told I'm going to turn out like the first two if I move out, and if I do move out, that sooner or later I'm going to come back with my tail between my legs begging for forgiveness. They just can't stand letting us go and live our own life. They are scared of losing us, but the way they are going about it is driving me nuts. I just want to have some time to think about what's good for me, not for everyone else, because it will help me to be more confident and not so scared, and to be my own person, not another part of someone else.

Things to do this week:

-Enrol in driving test.

-Ring Shena and get test papers.

-Do letters for employers.

-Send away letters.

Darius said he thinks he loves me. He wasn't completely sure before, because he hasn't felt it for any other or said it, and he was quite pessimistic about it. Then yesterday he said he loves me, so it is genuine, because if he didn't mean it he wouldn't say it because that's just who he is. I'm unsure about it, because I too haven't felt it. All I felt for other guys are crushes or attraction, but being with Darius is different. Darius said after saying that before, that he is quite certain that he loves me, but doesn't want me to tell anyone yet until he's gotten used to it and is more sure about it.

I really want to go to his mum's house during the midterm break for a holiday before work starts, because I have finished tech officially on Wednesday and completely on Friday. It really frustrated me that I have to argue with my parents about whether I can go or not. I'm 18! I really appreciated when my younger sister went and stood up for me by saying it was stupid about not letting me go. She says it is pathetic about them treating us like 4-year-olds. Well, they're not treating us like that, but they are very protective over us and it is especially hard when both your older sister and brother has set certain examples that your parents will expect you to turn out like. Lauren admits she made the wrong choice about moving to live with an ex-boyfriend, but it was her choice and she learnt the hard way, and anyway, she was plenty old enough – I think she was 21 at the time. Yes, because I had just turned sixteen and she's five years older than me. But back to my point, she still doesn't believe that living with a male is wrong, and I don't either, and my younger sister wouldn't either too, but it's not right in Mum and Dad's eyes, because they grew up in different times. Now it is quite alright, but not to them or the very strict Yugoslav family.

THURSDAY
5
JULY

On Sunday Darius and I left to go to New Plymouth to visit his mother, stepfather, and stepbrother. The trip took 5 hours and 15 minutes. The extra 15 minutes was because we went through Cambridge when we shouldn't have. It was funny.

When we got there Darius's mother and stepfather showed us around New Plymouth. It is a small city. We stayed till Wednesday and it was great fun. On Monday we climbed up Mt. Egmont to touch snow. For me and Darius's stepbrother, it was the first time we've ever seen real snow. I got some really great photos. That night we saw videos – 'Turner and Hooch', which I had already seen, and 'Rainman', which was excellent. Dustin Hoffman is a very, very good actor.

On Tuesday, Darius, his stepbrother, and I went and looked at the shopping centre, which was very big, much like the Manukau one. We also walked a bit around town, but decided to go back because it was raining. That night, also with Darius's mum, we saw 'Red October', which is an excellent movie with Sean Connery and Sam Neil acting in it. Sam Neil's a New Zealand actor.

On Wednesday, Darius and I left for a long drive home. We stopped off at the Waitomo Caves to see the glow worms and the caves. At the first cave I was so pissed off that I couldn't take photos, because I forgot my flash. But it didn't matter in the glow worm's cave, because you couldn't take photos there anyway. That cave I really enjoyed. We went on a little boat trip as well, through the cave to see the glow worms. I wanted to stay longer in New Plymouth, but it was lucky that my parents let me go at all, so I must be thankful.

Darius watched the Carpenter story with me when we got back home. He does love me definitely. He said so many times. He said that I am the first woman he has felt like this for. I'm scared he won't get into Auckland University next year, because he would have to go to Waikato University. I'm going to enrol for my driving test tomorrow and I'm going to start driving a car too, because if he does have to go down there I will be able to visit him and he can come up and see me. I love him too.

Darius's mother is a brilliant knitter. The stuff she knitted for her sons are so excellent, and she is really quick. I'm going to learn to knit too, so I can make beautiful things like that eventually, but it will be after a lot of practice.

I've got to get a job soon so I can quit Kendals and start properly saving for a car.

My younger sister is going to be a bridesmaid as well as me now for our older sister's wedding, because she was being a pain. I think she was jealous. The wedding is getting closer and closer, it's after my birthday.

Darius's birthday is soon, I've got to do something really excellent for him.

Darius wants to <u>marry</u> me. He said it yesterday after we had gone to a Peruvian restaurant with Nina and her boyfriend. It came as a real surprise, especially with the way he feels about marriage, but he said that he loves me so much, and I love him. Marriage is such a scary thought, because it's such a big step and a huge commitment to make. He said he knows that we are too young now so we can wait a couple of years, but he wants to live with me forever. For the rest of his life he wants to be with me. He said that he is lost without me, in those words. He said we should get engaged, then said it would be best if we don't say anything before my sister's wedding. Maybe next year is a good time to get engaged.

It is so scary. He said to think about it and that is what I'm doing. Thinking and writing. He is my first boyfriend.

I want to be with him. Maybe I'm too young to think about it now – I don't know. I love him. WOW! It's scary.

Darius loves me so much that, even though he's scared of marriage because of what happened with his parent's one, he still wants to marry me. WOW! Man, it was quite a surprise when he said that. <u>Marriage!</u> WOW!

I want to be with him now, right now. I love him. I love him!

211

Man, will Mum and Dad get a shock. I'd probably cry at my own wedding. Lauren's wedding is in two weeks from Saturday, and I can't wait. I want to catch the bouquet of flowers. Darius actually proposed to me! He said he would never betray me, and I won't betray him either.

PROS of marriage

_____

Love

Being together

Sharing everything

Children (later)

Freedom

Own home

Living together (might be different to live with?)

CONS of marriage

_____

Age – so young

Career

Income

Uncertainty. It's forever – big step – scary.

FRIDAY
7
SEPTEMBER

I am now nineteen.

I love Darius so much, and this is for real now. It's the type of realness that warrants a life together. Last night I had a really vivid dream. It was about Darius and I. I can't really remember where it was placed, but it was about us in a weird place with weird people, and I think we tried to get away, and Darius got caught in something magical and was turned into a seventeen-year-old, and so he didn't know me because he didn't know me at that age, so he was with another girl in a shower having sex and I was crying so much – like having lost my only love, and then someone told me how to change him back to twenty again by me hugging another guy. I was unsure about this, but I love Darius too much to let him go, so a guy came out, one who was after me, and we hugged and Darius changed back, and then the person who helped us told us, or me, that we won't remember any of this and so everything was back to normal, except for the girl who Darius was with at the age of seventeen, who had a baby and sent it away to another country and forgot about everything.

The other dream that came was about a whole lot of people being in a warehouse and I was with this Greek family who were going to perform in front of the crowd, and in this Greek family was a boy my age and he was flirting with me on stage, but so as no one else could see, but he started coming on heavy and I was trying to push him away from me so that Darius wouldn't see.

The other part of that dream was hazy, and was about us trying to go to the toilet, but people were trying to embarrass us by throwing water over the toilets and drenching us (this could have been related to my inability to go to the toilet properly for the past week). And another dream was about Darius and I walking a long way through the country and basically getting lost, then finding our way out by a motorway, which suddenly appeared and had other people walking along it. Then those people turned around, because they couldn't go any further, and we just ended up going towards the shops.

Dreams are really strange and right now they scare me. I can remember them so well and for a long time. I am writing at 11:00 pm at night about dreams that happened last night. These dreams scare me because they are confusing and they make me nervous, especially the first one when I thought Darius had betrayed me, which nearly tore me apart. Though, I knew I would do anything to get him back, including forgetting what had happened in the past.

I really love Darius and it would tear me apart if he betrayed me for real. He said he would never two-time me and that he loves me so much. I can honestly say I want to marry him and spend the rest of my life with him. But, it is so scary that I am trapped in this situation at home where I have to have permission for everything we do together. See, he believes that it is best to live together before marriage so we can test the waters before leaping in, but Mum and Dad believe that the latter is the best and I'm caught in between. I can't lose Darius no matter what; there is too much love on both sides for it to be ruined. I am the first girl Darius has ever loved. He said he made a commitment to me and I have made one to him too. We can never break that commitment or love or bonding.

A practice letter written for a CV (no date included)

Art is a way of life now. I have been doing it for as long as I can remember, and have carried it through high school and right into tech. At tech I acquired a graphics and design certificate. I enjoy graphic art very much, especially detailed and complicated works such as seen in illustration. Also, I enjoy visualising and have a good sense of what would look right in a lot of different medias. The subject of English, and everything that is classed under it, such as good communication on paper, is another interest for me. I enjoy writing and meeting people.

I have also gained School Certificate, Sixth Form Certificate as well as my Graphic Art Certificate. In addition, I have got a department diploma and I'm experienced on the Apple Mac and Wang computers in Pagemaker and Freehand. For my past-times I enjoy sport, which is karate, and at the moment I'm a green belt in training for a blue belt. I also enjoy badminton, running, and at present I'm a member of my local gym. I have enjoyed team sports in the past, such as touch rugby, netball, basketball, etc. I enjoy meeting and working with people. I can work well in a team situation as well as under high pressure, and have experienced tight deadlines with tech.

At the moment I am working at Kendals department store during the Christmas break, which was my part-time job during the year. I have also worked part-time at Garmers and in Lana's Coffee Lounge when I was younger. I am experienced with dealing with money and can budget well.

I am open-minded and am always ready to learn and take in other people's ideas and techniques. I get on well with my fellow workers and have always worked to the best of my ability.

Diary 1991

THURSDAY
21
FEBRUARY

I am really getting depressed about my job situation – zilch! I went for an interview on Wednesday at the brewery in East Tamaki for a graphic artist job, but I most likely won't get it. I just can't stand not having somewhere to go to. All my life I've had things done for me and places to go to every day. Please let me get this job! I was probably the youngest and least experienced person going for it. The most fucking introverted and shy shit there is. I wish I wasn't so shy. It sux. I need a job badly. I hate working at Kendals. The job sux, but the people are nice. I feel embarrassed working there, especially if someone I know comes in. I stress that it is only a part-time job. I know I shouldn't be ashamed of it, but I am. A shop assistant's job sux, it's demeaning. Like you're not good enough or talented enough to get anything else. I don't feel talented art wise at all. I'm too slow, so I don't feel talented. I'm ashamed of some of my work and why won't anyone hire me if I am talented. I need a job to go to, not a sleep in. Even when I'm overly pressured I feel better than I am feeling now.

I'm depressed.

FRIDAY
19
APRIL

Dear Diary,

It has been a while since I have written properly for you, and since then I've had many frustrations and aggravations in my pursuit of work. I went for an interview today and was really upset after I got home.

The interview was arranged by an employment agency and it was at a costume place. It was a very amateurish place. I had to walk there with my heavy folder and my Ken Wahl picture, and by the time I got there my back was drenched with sweat and my arm was ready to drop off.

The employer was a weird lady and the work looked far from what I'm looking for. I had to catch a taxi home and it cost $5. My stuff was just too heavy to carry back again.

I suppose, Diary, that if I get the job I will have to take it. But, I do not want to give up my job at the Ad Agency, where I work every Wednesday. I thought that since this job is close to home, and is from 12-7 pm, I might be able to work in the mornings at the Ad Agency, which is just for experience, not money, other than the bus fare they give me so I'm not losing anything by going there.

I'm also going for another job as an unarmed combat and self-defence instructor tomorrow.

Well, I'm going to get ready for work so I'll write later. And I promise, Diary, that I will write everything I think and feel and do in here, or I might get a padlocked diary for the serious stuff.

Dear Diary,

I have a lot of things that I wish to say in you about my past, future, and what I feel inside. Everything that I will write in you will be uncensored, unlike my other diaries in which I was too scared to write about the serious stuff just in case someone happened to read it, and so they contained only the trivial life of a frustrated teenager. I'm sure at the time it seemed serious enough to me, but it took on the form of a babbling teenage girl's memoirs. I do admit they contained some serious emotions and problems, but they were mainly hidden away in poems or riddles, so no one would understand what I was saying. I even read Darius one of my riddles while in New Plymouth, and he didn't work it out. Here's one part of the passage that I read to him.

"...the only boy supposed to carry on the name and pass it to his off-spring, of which he cannot do without killing his feelings. Feelings that caused rebellion, because of the difference and opposition it caused to one's parents. Parents hurt because of this different being that has abandoned tradition for his life in another sphere."

(A NOTE FROM THE AUTHOR – I cannot state who I was writing about and referring to in this riddle, as it would be a breach of their privacy. Therefore, I must blank out their name so their identity remains unknown. Sorry for the inconvenience and I hope you will understand)

The riddle was written about _____, who left home around the age of eighteen, because he's homosexual. His parents, I'm sure, are still hoping that he will come back and revert his sexual preferences to females. But how can he do that? You can't just change your sexual attitudes like that, or 'revert back' to something when there was nothing there in the first place. I'm sure that if someone was to tell me that I should have sexual fantasies about females I would think that they were gross and I'm sure _____ feels the same in his case. But, I'm not saying that I want him to be homosexual, and yes, I am hoping he will be like an average male who has fantasies of Elle McPherson or Michele Pfeiffer, but I know that is unrealistic thinking. And anyway, it's none of my business, it's his life not mine. I will love him no matter what.

I don't see him that much anymore, except for special occasions, so it now doesn't come into my mind that often. But, what comes into my mind now, or what I should say occupies my mind 24 hours a day both consciously and unconsciously is my hunt for a proper job. Continually over the past year I have been knocked back by one employer after another. It has been really frustrating, humiliating, and it hurts. I have tried hard, but after one knock-back too many I have become lazy and unwilling. This is true, because why am I sitting here now writing to you instead of walking those streets looking for work? Laziness or cowardliness?

Next Thursday on Dad's birthday, I have an interview for a job for a new company, and I hope it goes well.

Dear Diary,

I love Darius! I really do. He really moved me on the phone tonight. I love him so much! He was really down in the dumps. I think he was partly crying. I get that way too. He said he missed me. I couldn't say much because my mum was in the same room as me. I really want to marry Darius, but he's changed his mind and doesn't want to marry. He said that it wasn't because of me. He said that if he would ever marry it would be me, but he won't, but he said that anything is possible. I'm praying that I can change his mind again like the last time. I really love and care about him. The problem is that he came from a broken marriage and he saw how much hurt it caused. His idea of marriage is that it's a prelude to an inevitable divorce. I don't believe in that.

It's scaring me the way that he is talking. I know that he loves me, but university and other things are becoming too much for him. He has to support himself, which means he works a lot, as well as doing his university studies. He is so hard working.

Things are becoming totally jumbled for me. Too many different things go through my eyes and head every day, but seem meaningless.

I haven't got a job in graphic art yet (full-time) and it's causing chaos. I have almost, but not completely, lost interest in karate. It's scary, but I believe that I was better as a beginner, because I had spirit and determination. I didn't worry about getting hurt then, but now my fighting skills are poor because of this fear of getting hurt.

I have a karate camp this weekend, so I must use it to get my spirit back up. I can't continue karate if my spirit hits rock bottom.

I feel like I must always be doing something or else I might start feeling confused and worrisome. So far I've had no great achievement this year, besides getting my driver's license. That is great in a way, but what I mean is that I want to achieve something that is really wonderful, eg. getting a job, getting engaged, etc.

I feel real lonely sometimes, even though I have Darius and my family. I don't have any real close girlfriends. Shena is my friend, but she isn't close enough to know my secrets, wants, and expectations. I need a friend who knows those things. I must ring Penelope up. I hope she's not too entangled in Simon so that she has no time left for me, because I really need a best (girl) friend.

I believe you make things out of life how you want it if you really try hard. That's my problem. I haven't tried hard enough and it is a fault. I must plan things better. If I want to succeed I must become more assertive and hard-working, and it is going to start tomorrow. From now on every night I will write down one success, emphasis on success, that I have achieved during that day. And if I fail on anything I must write it down too, so that I will remember everything about it and will <u>never</u> do it again, and will learn from it. I will also write what happened during that day and how I felt about it. I will carry you with me, Diary. Also, I must find a padlocked box for you.

I must be better than Nick at karate, Michael at self-defence, and always love everyone for themselves, and not listen to petty prejudices people spread.

Dear Diary,

I now have an Omni cheque account. I went to the shopping centre today during my lunch hour to look for a sports bra for the karate camp, but I decided against getting one in the end. Therefore, I had half an hour spare, so I decided on getting a cheque account. Either tomorrow or Friday I will pick the cheque book up.

Today at self-defence and unarmed combat fighting, I did my first lot of sparring and it was heaps of fun. I also learnt how to do leg sweeps. There are thick mats on the floor, so we don't get hurt when we get taken down.

After that I went back to Darius' house for a while, then home. I'll tell you more about it later. I'm getting tired now.

See ya!

MONDAY
27
MAY

Sorry about not writing sooner. I've been very busy lately. I went on the karate camp and have worked for two weeks at Kendals (yuck!). And I've had numerous amounts of activities on.

Tomorrow I'm going for an interview at the local newspaper after a long time of ringing them up. Anthony, a friend from high school, the one who left for journalism school, works at the Manukau branch. He tipped me off that the artist at the local branch had just left.

Yesterday I went to Rainbow's End with Darius and it was fun. I'll tell you about everything later on in more detail when I have time.

Goodnight!

Dear Diary,

I love Darius so much. I want to do more for him. He won't have a part-time job soon, because his work is trying to cut staff off, which means that Darius will be in real financial difficulty, and I don't know what to do. I really want to help him without hurting his feelings, because he is really independent.

I love him so much. I want to be with him all the time. But his views about marriage and religion are so different from mine. He's an Atheist and so he doesn't believe in what I believe in. He also told me he won't get married, but once he proposed to me when we were younger, so I have a glimmer of hope that he might propose again.

I want to help and do as much for him as I can, and more.

(My teenage diaries finish here as the next diary extract is after I've turned 20. But since my diaries continue sporadically until 1993 I will include them)

Dear Diary,

I'm really worried about Darius not getting a job during the summer holidays, because if he can't find work in Auckland he will go up to live with his father during that time, which is from just before December to March (3 months). I don't think I can take that unless I visit him all the time, which will be very expensive. I'm really praying that he will find a job here. I love him so much.

Darius has exams now, so I won't see him for a few weeks, which I pray will fly by fast because after only a couple of days I miss him.

I've seen a lot more of Shena lately. On Saturday I went to Hunter's Plaza with her and her family, and also I saw a video with her and her boyfriend at night. The other day we drove around and we talked about flatting together. I think it's a great idea. She said when we are around 21 would be a good time. I don't know whether I can take much more of living with my younger sister. She is really unbearable to live with sometimes. She is so rude. Also, I need independence. I need to be able to cope on my own and learn, but I am really scared to tell Mum and Dad that I want to flat. I am 20 now and feel too babied. I feel so stupid, literally, as well as naive. I know nothing about flatting and taking care of myself. I know I'll miss home a hell of a lot, but will get used to it. I need to experience life for itself, not something censored all of the time. I still get told what to do at 20 as if I'm younger, as if I was not an adult yet. I feel so smothered. I'm still shy and quiet, unsure of myself, because I'm being treated like a kid and I'm too scared to hurt my parents' feelings and say that I want to move out. I'm scared Darius will leave me if they won't give me space. Eventually everything will come to a climax and I will have to decide what to do and choose. I feel guilty that I want my younger sister to leave and so they will want me to leave, too. Nina's not really ready to leave at her age, it should be me leaving. I can afford it. I have a stable job, and Nina is unemployed, because she quit her job. I think I should move out next year, but trust me and my gutlessness, I won't. I want to. It should be fun living with Shena, because she is a lot like me and we should get along well together under the same roof. Of course we'll probably need a third person, another girl obviously, because my parents would throw a fit otherwise. I don't want to hurt them, I just need space. I've had this feeling that things aren't right together anymore, because we're all grown up now, the kids, so I need to start the second phase of life, the independent learning, experiencing phase. It should be so fun. I feel that Darius thinks I'm still a kid and I feel that way too. The only way I will grow up is to experience life on my own, away from the family. Of course I will visit them heaps. I hope everything will work out fine.

MONDAY
4
NOVEMBER

It's November! I can't believe how everything is going so fast. But, I bet these two weeks won't go fast enough for me. Darius has exams this week and next, and I haven't seen him for a week because of his study. I am really missing him. It would be almost 3 weeks from when I last saw him to when I will see him next. It's driving me nuts. Also, what else is really driving me nuts is that he doesn't know whether he will have a job during the Christmas break. I'm really, really praying that his job will still let him work for them. Hopefully, he will find out on Friday. I'm really praying hard for him. I love him so much. I really mean this. Darius is the first guy that I have ever loved. I love my dad and brother, but that's a different type of love. A family love.

I've finally got a new two-piece swimsuit, and it's really nice. It's bright light blue with little yellow flowers as the design. Next, I just need a tan and then I will put some colour through my hair. I might be giving a sunbed a go at my gym next week. I've never been on one before.

I've brought practically all my Christmas presents. I got a lot of them from the Craft Show and the Expo centre on Sunday. I went with Shena. The stalls were brilliant, I could have bought the lot it was that good. There were heaps and heaps of different stalls there, all brilliant, some more so than others.

I went to Guy Fawkes on Saturday with my friends to see the fireworks display. It was alright, nothing great.

Goodnight.

Diary 1992

THURSDAY
2
APRIL

Dear Diary,

What do I want to do with my life? I want and need to become famous. I don't know exactly why I want this, but I feel I need to be loved and well-known by a lot of people. I feel that it'll give me my purpose for being alive.

Why am I alive? It's hard to explain the feeling that you are the only one out there. I can't explain it. Why was I put here: in this family I love, this country I love, and in this world? What is my importance to be granted life? What am I supposed to do?

I'm impatient in ways. I want to become famous while I'm still young. What will I become famous for? Art? Art is the only thing that I can do outstanding. But I feel that it's still not good enough. I need to improve. I don't have that many good pictures. The Indian picture is the only outstanding one I have done.

Why do I want to be famous, why the need? Is it because I am a shy, withdrawn person who wishes to break free and live it up? Is it because I want to be embraced by the world? I wish I could find my career, my meaning in life. It's hard to explain. I really need that meaning desperately. I felt there was something special waiting out there for me while I was still at school. I see something special for Darius too. Prime Minister of New Zealand.

I need to put my body in the best condition it will ever be in. I feel I will be young forever. I am scared of growing old. There is not enough time to live life to its fullest so I must start soon.

Saturday: Swim   Sunday: Karate
     Gym   ?
     Sauna   ?
     Sunbed   I need exercise

I love Darius, but I'm unsure of the future. Will he ever want to get married to me? Ever? He said he doesn't want to be married – not just to me, but he said if he ever would, it would be me. I'm unsure. I think the reason he asked me the first time when we were younger was that he'd drunk a bit too much wine at the restaurant. Wine can bring out strong emotions, and with Darius it makes him very romantic. He probably got carried away in the moment. I probably did too, even though I didn't have any of the wine. Instead, I would've been caught up with how lovely he was being. Darius is so lovely. Fingers and toes crossed he will change his mind again.

On a different note, I want to travel. To see places, to be welcomed by smiling, happy faces. Faces that are fascinated by me.

I am a big Queen fan. I think Roger Taylor is gorgeous and the group brilliant. Is that why I want to see England, because they are from there?

I can be a very obsessive person sometimes, which drives me nuts.

Why me? There is a reason why and I will find out.

I love you.

But, these things are nothing. They are childish, but heartfelt babblings of a young person.

(AGED 21)

I'm upset. I'm not working at the newspaper anymore. I haven't been there since the end of September. I was fired. My boss didn't think I was good enough. Darius said I should've had my boss up for being fired, because it wasn't my fault I had to order some work from the computer people. Things can't always be done by hand and, if anything, I think I got the blame for the girl who was with me. I'm stupid; I should've stood up for myself. It was a different boss from the one who hired me, and she was always on my back, she even took my office away not long after my other boss left. That was partly my fault due to doing some other drawings during the slow period, but I bucked up and did my work, but I think she thought I was too young. Maybe my attitude sucked, I don't know, but it sucked the way I was just let go like that without actually doing anything wrong. All I did was ask the computer guys to do a heading, THAT'S ALL, because I was asked by a salesperson. I really did get shafted.

And now I'm working for a crummy $7.50 an hour at a lunch bar for 25 hours a week.

The only thing that's happened to me that was excellent is that I'm engaged to Darius. The day after my 21st birthday party he proposed to me! He really did and in such a loving way. I won't tell you how, that is only for me and him to remember, but it was so heartfelt. I said yes straight away!

We're getting married!

Though, I'm not happy that he wants to stay at his mum's place in New Plymouth for the whole of the university holidays, which lasts around 3½ months. I don't want to be without him for that long. It's really upsetting me. But we are engaged now, so we will find a way around it.

Diary 1993

THURSDAY
28
JANUARY

The trees at Auckland University are beautiful, and so are the gorgeous little sparrows fighting for my bread.

The traffic travelling to and from here is absolutely horrific and is the worst part of the day. The parking is alright, until the students come back, then it will be a bigger problem than the traffic.

The work at the shop isn't for me. Sometimes it's alright, then other times it is so boring. I wish that I was drawing instead.

When the students get back, the shop will be chaotic. I don't mind that part so much. It will be the parking that will be worrying me.

Letters to Darius

(These appear to be practice letters, both dates unknown. The first one was probably written while Darius was staying at his mother's place during the Christmas break.)

Dear Darius,

How's everything going? Working at the bookshop is okay. I didn't get that job that I wanted though. They said that I got close, but they chose someone older. I have sent away for that job at Manukau Tech.

The drama students practice outside the bookshop. They are so strange, and they make a hell of a noise.

My cans picture is going really well, but really slow. I have got some more art ideas, so that's good. The bookshop has some excellent art books.

The traffic going to and from town is disgusting sometimes. I'm giving Nina a lift in and back now. I park at the student car parks for only a dollar a day, so at least that's cheap.

On Friday, Mum and I are going to look for my wedding dress pattern.

There is a carnival for some Chinese event going on, and it will be open until 2 am in the morning.

(Letter cuts off.)

(This letter relates to the possibility of Darius getting a job in Wellington, which is about a ten hour drive from Auckland.)

To Darius,

I really love you and really want to make things work out. I've been having a think about things and believe I was being selfish thinking that you will stay in Auckland with me. I won't stand in the way of your career and I want to assist it. If you decide to go to Wellington during my course I won't bother you. We can see each other in our holidays and just bear it out for 2 years, then I will come down to Wellington. That's if I get into Auckland University. Two years will be a drop in the ocean in our marriage, even though it won't seem like that at the time.

I'm sorry that sometimes I'm frustrating, because I keep things to myself a lot. I will try and tell you what I think from now on when you ask or when I feel like saying something.

I think you're absolutely wonderful.

(A letter found in my diary, which was written to my friend. It was messy, so was probably a practice one.)

Dear Penelope,

Hi! I bet you didn't think I would write. I didn't either. I'm terrible, aren't I?

Well, lots of things have happened since you were last here. I've got a full-time job with lots of overtime, and I mean lots! I'm working at a clothing warehouse. I'm doing approximately 10 ½ hours a day and a half a day on Saturday. Money's not so good, but I've got no choice. It's a real monotonous job, but the people are very nice. All I'm doing is pricing clothes and putting them on hangers. Whoopee! (Drink in the sarcasm).

I'm hoping to keep it till the beginning of February, but I'll probably have it till Christmas, because that's when most of the temporaries finish.

And now for Art School. I had an interview for the art school on the other side of town, but not for the university one. Well, what they haven't seen is their loss. Obviously, I'm not devastated, just peeved about not getting an interview. But I can't say it wasn't expected with their reputation. Anyway, I don't find out about whether I've gotten into the art school until the end of November. I don't think I got into the 2nd year, but I think I might have a chance for the first year. The guy at the interview asked me why I didn't want to do the first year and old big mouth me said that the fee was too high, and I forgot to say that it was because I thought that I might have enough qualifications and experience to get into the 2nd year. He sounded keen on me applying for 1st year. But, I thought that the interview was very unprofessionally done. Slapdash, in and out. The only picture I could tell that he liked was my 'Canned' one.

Anyway, so far the wedding preparations are going alright. I have my first dress fitting this coming Friday. I've got practically all my material for the dress. I still need to get my material for my after wedding suit, but I've already decided what material to get. I'm thinking of making it myself. Well, I will certainly try. The dressmaker costs $15 per hour.

Mike's doing the invitations for me. It's part of his wedding gift. So they should be sent off in December.

Darius has his last exam on Saturday. At last! He can't wait. Then after that we will go off with Sebastian to see their father, and stay the night. Thank God he decided not to go to Wellington, which is a HUGE relief.

1994

Darius and I got married.

EPILOGUE

"Darius" and I are still married, and have two children, one of whom is coming up to the age I was at the beginning of the diaries. And while reading over my teenage dreams and aspirations, I was surprised to discover that I had achieved many of my goals, such as becoming an author. I have published a few books prior to this one and after reading about my teenage idea for the story *'Town Without Pity'* I may actually write it.

I have also worked as an artist and have obtained a Bachelor of Arts degree in Italian Studies and Art History (of which I won an award for being the top undergraduate student in Art History for my 3rd year). Additionally, I obtained an Honours degree in Art History, and have won some awards for my art as well as having painted an important commission for the Dalmatian Cultural Society's 150 year anniversary. This work (a set of four large canvases) depicts 150 years of the Dalmatian people (from the coast of Croatia) being in New Zealand. The finely detailed works put together are the dimensions of a queen size bed and took several months to paint. The current Prime Minister of New Zealand, John Key, unveiled it.

In relation to my other activities, although I'm not as sports mad as I once was, I still love it and run regularly. I have completed a couple of marathons, as well as a thirty-K run and quite a number of half marathons. And I would absolutely love to run the New York Marathon, which I've heard is quite an experience.

In karate, the highest belt I achieved was a brown belt with a black stripe, which is one below a black belt. I should've gone for my black belt, but lost interest when my club dwindled to very small numbers. However, later on, around 2006, I found the club had reformed and returned for about a year or so, taking my children to participate. My daughter achieved an orange belt before we moved. However, where karate left off, soccer filled the void, of which I have always had an interest. I have coached for a number of years and will run onto the field if someone needs a goalie, although I prefer to watch my daughter play instead.

If you wish to learn more about me, my art, and my writing, follow the links on the next page.

Author Facebook Page:
https://www.facebook.com/pages/Marita-A-Hansen/113130742120676

Graffiti Heaven Page:
https://www.facebook.com/graffitiheaven.novel

Blog Site: http://maritaahansen.blogspot.co.nz/

Amazon Author Page:
http://www.amazon.com/Marita-A.-Hansen/e/B005H5W79K/ref=ntt_athr_dp_pel_1

Goodreads' Author Page:
http://www.goodreads.com/author/show/5129673.Marita_A_Hansen

Artslant Page:
http://www.artslant.com/global/artists/show/74433-marita-hansen

Twitter Name: @MaritaAHansen

Printed in Great Britain
by Amazon

40436240R00148